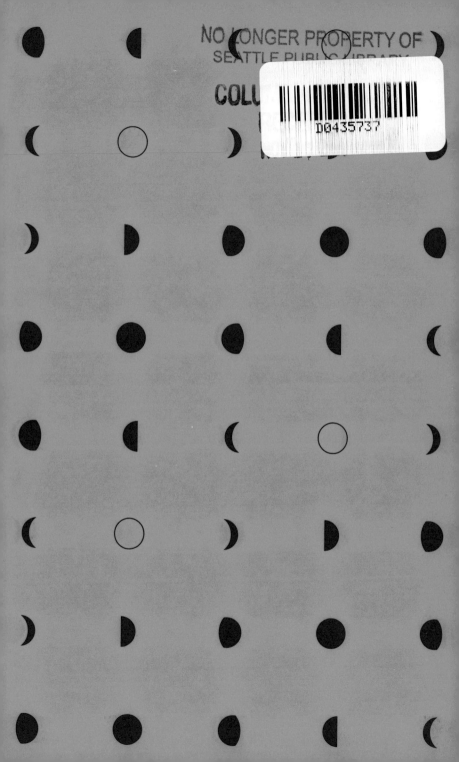

Praise for
ENCHANTMENTS

"Hilariously conversational, deceptively deep, and phenomenally illustrated, *Enchantments* will blow your mind and make you laugh while imparting expert knowledge of witchcraft and why it's so needed today."
—NATASHA LYONNE, actress and producer

"Part memoir, part recipe book, and part poetry collection, *Enchantments* lets readers in on the great secret of all witchcraft—that being a witch is about being free to be yourself. In a spirit of collaboration and community and with limber humor and wit, Spalter empowers all of us to be the best magical practitioners we can be. A future classic for both new and experienced witches, or anyone in the mood for a little divination."
—DOROTHEA LASKY, author of *Milk* and co-creator of Astro Poets

"All the things you've always wanted to know about becoming a witch but were afraid to ask! We can all use more magic in our lives in these trying times, and *Enchantments* will help us get started. Now who wants to join my coven and cast some spells?"
—Kimya Dawson, singer-songwriter (*Juno* soundtrack/Moldy Peaches)

ENCHANTMENTS

ENCHANTMENTS

A MODERN WITCH'S GUIDE TO SELF-POSSESSION

MYA SPALTER

ILLUSTRATED BY
CAROLINE PAQUITA

NEW YORK

Published in the United States by Lenny,
an imprint of Random House, a division of
Penguin Random House LLC, New York.

LENNY and colophon are trademarks of Penguin Random House LLC.

LIBRARY OF CONGRESS CATALOGING-IN-PUBLICATION DATA

Names: Spalter, Mya, author.
Title: Enchantments: a modern witch's guide to self-possession / Mya Spalter.
Description: First Edition. | New York: Lenny, 2018.
Identifiers: LCCN 2018007307 | ISBN 9780525509653 |
ISBN 9780525509660 (ebook)
Subjects: LCSH: Occultism. | Witchcraft. | Magic. | Astrology.
Classification: LCC BF1411 .S725 2018 | DDC 130—dc23
LC record available at https://lccn.loc.gov/2018007307

Illustrations by Caroline Paquita

Printed in the United States of America on acid-free paper

randomhousebooks.com

2 4 6 8 9 7 5 3 1

First Edition

Book design by Elizabeth A. D. Eno

To the Moon

Contents

Introduction

In which I introduce myself and tell how I ended up working at Enchantments, New York City's oldest witchcraft store.

I was bald and nineteen years old. I couldn't find my bra. It was my sophomore year at college. I needed a job. The $20 my mom would give me once a week was just enough to keep me in French cigarettes, croissants, and pretension. Pretension and smoking were much cheaper habits to maintain in the year 2000 than at present writing. I lived at 31 Union Square West, which sounds real fancy, but my roommates and I managed to make a squalor of it. We smoked constantly and threw knives at the walls. When the weather was nice we'd lie out on the antique limestone window ledges, counting on the awning of the restaurant below to act as a net should the trick go sideways.

I was bald because (a) I listened to a lot of Ani DiFranco at the time. Like, a lot. Like, enough for it to concern people who cared about me. And (b) my ex had just told me to shut up about shaving my head because I was never going to do it and she hates it when people talk about shit they're never gonna do. I had no choice, really. The jazz boys upstairs had clippers. It was on. By *on*, I mean my hair was on the carpeted floor of our kitchenette, later to be collected into a plastic bag and stored in a Smashing Pumpkins CD box-set box. So now you know everything you need to know about me in my youth.

But the baldness makes a special kind of sense to me now. Most religious orders require some sort of tonsorial process for novices. A shaved head is a line in the sand. What came before is gone, and in that moment of separation from the past, the future can begin.

I'd spent most weekends in high school moodily mooning around the East Village, so I'm amazed I had never stumbled upon Enchantments before the day I came through looking for a job. I'd spent the afternoon ducking my bald head into every shop that looked open.

I finally arrived at a grungy little storefront with a dinged-up sheet-metal crescent moon hanging outside like a shingle. I stepped through the door and into a billow of smoke issuing from a little cauldron in the hand of a middle-aged white lady with Peppermint Patty hair and a wolves-howling-at-the-moon sweatshirt over a turtleneck. A classic look. I asked her if they needed any help around the shop, and she said, "Whatever you're putting out, sister, it's working! You're hired!" So mote it be.

For the next few years, I worked behind the counter pouring oils and carving candles at the city's oldest witchcraft store. Back then, we worked at a pretty leisurely pace. It was a very different neighborhood. Most of the people who came in knew what they were there for. They had a list of herbs or a special item they dutifully picked up every week; these were folks who kept altars vigilantly in dedication to a particular deity, or those who depended on the favor of certain fickle forces for their livelihood, like the sex workers and dancers who made their living off the trusty spells that lured their customers and encouraged them to make it rain.

More than fifteen years later I'm working at Enchantments again, and we're busier than ever. What the people need now is less often material and less often related to sex work. As you may know, the East Village is now bougie as fuck. As of this writing, the price of a coffee has exceeded the price of a subway ride by more than a dollar. That was never supposed to happen. But what we're seeing more and more often are young people who are very eager and interested in getting an intention candle but don't seem to have the first idea of what their intention is. This troubles me. I mean, how do you know you want a candle if you don't know what you want it for? Enchantments sells candles, oils, herbs, and incense for nearly every purpose, from weight loss to, I dunno, sending a message of love to a departed family pet. The only limits are your own good sense and imagination, two qualities that frequently seem to be lacking.

Instead of bemoaning the situation, I figured I'd be better off making a resource for the folks who walk into the store like, "What's this all about?" while gesturing at the fragrant, glittery clutter around them. This book is my answer: a document that sums up the sort of things we wish we could explain about modern witchcraft in its many forms, for people who don't have the desire or opportunity to hang around the shop all day listening to us witches cackle, beat each other with wooden spoons, and kibitz our way into the great oral history of modern magic and witchery. That would be the best way to learn this stuff, but we're so busy these days and it's a small store. Luckily, this book is huge! There's enough room for all of you in it.

But why should you care?

Maybe because witchcraft's focus on honing one's personal power and drawing strength from a variety of sources—from the wealth of ancient and living traditions, from one's own ancestors, from the Earth itself—and then using that power to heal our fractured selves and culture, foster growth, and harbor life is as resonant now as ever. Because the percentage of young people involved in organized religion has never been lower, yet the innate human need for ritual and a sense of connection to something outside of ourselves isn't going anywhere. If anything, it's been brought closer to the surface by the stark horror of our national condition. Because at a moment when the rights of women and gender-nonconforming people are under increased and constant attack from institutions of power, a non-hierarchical, goddess-centered style of spirituality has a markedly increased appeal. Because we're in a moment in which a lot of people are feeling a greater urgency toward practices that can offer some way toward meaning, peace, and self-possession.

Finding ways to access your own intuition is the very center of witchcraft practice, as I see it. If you're guided by your intuition, you can't really avoid magic. Every language has words that describe the uncanny ability of someone to manifest their will, but I think it might be useful here to use the term "self-possession," both because of its accepted meaning (i.e., bringing all of one's strengths to bear, being unswayed by other people's opinions, etc.) and because of the possession part (as in being entirely enthralled to a spirit), but in this case it's a DIY operation. You can enthrall yourself to your own spirit. Haunt your own damn house.

But we'll talk more about all that soon. Let's skip to the part where I tell you that I'm not an expert. I mean, who the hell am I, right? I'm sure I know less practical information about witchcraft than a lot of my coworkers at Enchantments. But the magic part is that I don't have to be an expert in order to show people how to build their own practice out of whatever they have to hand. I've been doing it all my life. I used magic to help me find my true love, not to mention my truly lovely yet affordable apartment in Brooklyn. And if you're reading this, my spell to help me get my writing career off the ground is coming along quite nicely.

This book will introduce you to a magical approach to life and give you a tour of a strange place that is very familiar to me. I like to think of Enchantments as a microcosm of the greater magical ecosystem, a place where witches, Pagans, and polytheists of all stripes come to gather their seven-day candles and other articles of devotion. In Part One, I'll tell you about some of the commonly used witchy implements and how you might employ them. In Part Two, we'll look at some of the ways you can combine these elements to further your own magical intentions.

When I say magical, I'm really talking about an attitude: a magical person embraces the presupposition that you can materially impact the condition of your life by setting a goal or intention, ritualizing that intention, visualizing the outcome of your desire, and letting it happen. We carry out these processes constantly throughout our lives. The impulses that travel from our brains to our body parts are invisible but undeniable manifestations of this principle. If all's well with the body, we intend a movement and magically/electrically/mechanically it's carried out by the corresponding body part. There's a slight mysterious poof of something, an unseen spark ignites from . . . somewhere . . . and then, look! My toes wiggled! Just like I wanted them to! The fact that I understand the mechanics behind it doesn't make it any less of a miracle. And that's what witches do: we look for magic, for divinity, in everything. What's more, we allow ourselves to find it, even in the seemingly mundane. Odds are you're already using the most basic tools and practices of magic in your regular life. It might be more fun to be intentional about it. Let's go have some fun.

Part One

WITCHY
IMPLEMENTS

Chapter 1

WHERE THE MAGIC HAPPENS, OR ALTARS

Now that we're well acquainted, I'll show you my altars. The altar is an area of your home that's devoted to your spiritual life. It can serve as a workspace for building your spells, or as a tiny temple for honoring a deity, saint, intention, or concept. The important part is that your altar is a dedicated space. Most people who practice witchcraft or another polytheistic worship have at least one altar in their home. But no pressure. Even people who aren't spiritually inclined seem to be able to get down with the beneficial function of an altar as a place to model peace and balance in our lives. It's aspirational.

If you don't already have a designated altar, find an uncluttered area where you can place items of spiritual significance to you: photos of departed loved ones, plants, postcards, paintings, crystals, mirrors, beads and jewelry, flowers, shells, stones, miscellaneous items of sentimental value. Go nuts. I wish I could come over and help you with this part. It's my favorite. I actually have a dream of starting a business called Spalter's Altars, where I go into people's homes and help them assemble altars out of items they already have or that we could go find at a yard sale or the dollar store. One of the principles of magic that I appreciate the most is the notion that you have what you need all around you. It's just up to you to be sharp enough to see it.

The items you collected for your altar are now to be considered ritual items. Ritual items are set apart from your other possessions, and you take special care with them. By "ritual," I mean an elevated habit—that is, a habit that has some symbolic meaning. Humans love ritual; we'll make a ritual out of anything. We've all wished on an eyelash, blown out birthday candles after chanting a little song, knocked on wood, or blessed someone who sneezed. We can't get enough of ritual, because it resonates with something deep in our human condition. Performing a prescribed action with the knowledge that you're part of a tradition is really powerful. It's an opportunity to inhabit a less mundane frame of mind. But we don't always realize our own agency to create and curate new and personal rituals, to respectfully draw from different practices to cobble together our own unique way to feel connected. Your altar can be a physical representation of what that process looks like for you.

I take immeasurable pleasure in making and maintaining my altars. Beyond my primary altar, every windowsill and plant pot in my house contains some semi-intentional collection of magical crap, so I'm always ready to create an altar to suit my mood or intention. I use whatever I have to hand at any moment: a feather, two marbles, a die turned meticulously to a particular side, broken statuary arranged to appear somewhat less broken, small plastic animals, sea glass and precious stones, widowed earrings, minuscule pinwheels, loose change, mica flakes and dried-up cherry blossoms, golden bobby pins and tiny crystal cordial glasses. I haven't yet applied the life-changing magic of tidying up, or whatever you call it, but I'm worried it wouldn't work on me because I truly love and viscerally enjoy every magpie sequin and pottery shard.

My one word of caution as you set up your altar is fire safety! You have to be so careful with candles and incense. If it's not safe to burn things on your altar, do it in a sink, or in a tub, or on the stovetop. Don't burn the house down, dummy.

Often for me, practicing solo as I do, the process of creating the altar *is* the ritual. Sometimes building the tiny, beautiful, sympathetic world of my altar, populated with all of the tiny talismans that bolster my intention, suffused with the sights and smells associated with the feeling I mean to provoke, can be a whole spell in itself.

With that in mind, let's explore the altar setups suggested by some Wiccan liturgy, as it's meant to cover all the bases, and then I'll show and tell how I choose to vary from that, to give you some ideas on how to create your own altars.

DO WHAT YOU FEEL.

I refer to Wiccan and Neo-Pagan traditions a lot in this book. Mostly because that's what I'm most familiar with from working at Enchantments, and through that work I've found that the traditions compiled under the name Wicca or modern Paganism host a lot of useful language for discussing matters of universal spiritual significance: the need to create sacred space, make real our connection to the Earth, wonder about our place in the universe, and connect with divinity. Wicca is a special blend of European folk cultures and some transliterations of Mesopotamian, Sumerian, Babylonian, and Egyptian deities and beliefs, but a lot of Pagans will honor any form of divinity that will sit still long enough. I intend no pun in saying that I'm enchanted by the texture and detail of these composite spiritual practices. I feel at home in traditions that are explicitly, consciously evolving human creations. They're roomy enough for my broad concept of the divine. I also find that modified versions of some Wiccan practices can be applied to lend a little structure to any self-guided practice you want to create. In straight-up Wiccan traditions, as opposed to the Wicca-ria-pop-magic-Jewish-Hoodoo that I do, the ritual items of the altar are more prescribed than my tchotchkes and family photos. That's not to say that they're dogmatic about it; it's just that some of the Wiccan ritual items are the props necessary to act out the processes that their liturgy calls for. Still, it's worth noting that rule number one in *A Witches' Bible* (which is a real book that you can read if Wicca interests you) is: Do what feels right to you. In the end, your altar or ritual might not bear much resemblance to the original, but that's just the point.

The way I look at it, an altar is like a temple in miniature, a diorama if you will, that contains small representations of the different types and directions of energy, roughly categorized as elements: earth, air, fire, water, and a fifth, ineffable thing, spirit, the animating force, often represented by the image of some deity.

In Wicca, the water element is represented by the ritual cup, or *chalice*, which is just the Christian word for cup. Earth is represented by a *pentacle*, or five-pointed star, constructed of a natural substance, like wood or metal. Air is often represented by an *athame*, a ceremonial witch knife, usually dark-handled (as opposed to the *boline*, a traditional white-handled witch knife used for everyday things like cutting herbs or carving), or by a sword (if you have that kind of space and you like LARPing). The fire element is represented by a *wand*. Wands are usually about a foot long, give or take, composed of wood, metal, precious stones, or some combination thereof.

Why these items, you might ask? They correspond to the suits of the Minor Arcana in the tarot (see Chapter 11), and their symbolic role on the altar is informed by a similar logic. The cup (water) is a mystical shorthand for the emotions, while the pentacle (earth) references foundational matters of physical practicality, labor, and money. Air, represented by the blade, is meant to indicate the uncanny quality of thought and language as tangible forces in the world, cutting through space. Which, incidentally, is what people actually do with their blades in ritual: point them as if to cut through the air, thereby directing energy. Wands (fire) are used similarly for directing energy, and in Wiccan liturgy they are meant to symbolize one's deeds and actions. But there's a lot of room for interpretation, and some folks prefer to reverse the two and use wands to represent air and thought and swords to represent fire and action. Arguing the point is a more academic exercise than I am interested in here, and since I don't personally use either of these symbols to represent the elements on my altar, the fine distinctions don't trip me up too much. You shouldn't let them trip you up, either. It's all about what resonates best with your style.

I love to discover the purpose and reasoning behind the ritual choices that other people make, but what excites me about magic and witchcraft is figuring out the nature of my *own* reasoning, and making my *own* ritual choices. My way represents water with . . . water. In some kind of vessel, of course, but I don't keep one in particular for the purpose, even though I just told you that your ritual items should be set aside for spiritual work only. *I do what I want!* I tend to choose the vessel to suit the day, the mood, the purpose I have in mind at the moment that I'm setting up. I have two of my great-grandmother's champagne glasses, and they can become chalices whenever I desire. If I'm working on some kind of new apartment spell for a friend, I have been known to use a mug that looks like the classic New York "We Are Happy to Serve You" coffee cup

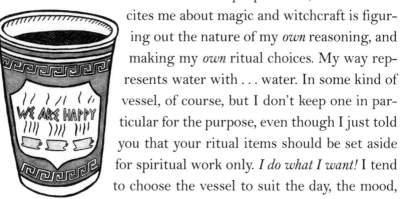

because it reminds me of the three of cups in tarot, a card that often represents sharing in joyful abundance with friends. But I only mix it up like that because I love hunting around for the perfect little thing. You might not! In which case, it is totally fine to just rock the same altar items no matter what you're doing.

I represent earth in a complementary vessel (coffee can, flowerpot, what have you) filled with salt or dirt. And I represent air with incense (since it's air that you can see and smell), which also requires some form of incense burner, cauldron, or ashtray in which to safely burn stick, cone, resin, or powder incense.

SMOKING IS COOL.

So many types of incense to choose from!

First, there's the kind we hand-make at Enchantments: **powder incense**. We make ours with a wood base, typically an extra-fine sawdust that absorbs whatever essential oils you add to it, and releases their scent when burned. The kind of wood base we use these days is treated with saltpeter so it burns pretty well if you just run a lit match through a spoonful of the powder in a heatproof dish, like an ashtray, or even a seashell.

Resins are hardened droplets of tree sap that release their scent when they melt on top of a hot surface. Frankincense, myrrh, amber, copal, and benzoin are all resins commonly used as incense.

Stick incense is powdered incense or resin affixed to a stick that burns evenly like a little fuse to keep the powder layer lit.

Cone incense is the same idea as stick incense, only compressed and molded into a shape that promotes a slow, controlled burn from the tip down.

If you want to burn resins, or a lot of powdered incense at once, you'll need some charcoal. Incense-burning charcoal is kind of like the briquette you would use for a BBQ, but tiny and shaped like a hockey puck. You hold it between the fingers of one hand while holding a lighter under the opposite side, until it begins to catch and spark. Once the sparks get halfway across the disk you'd better put it down somewhere before you burn your hand. A small cauldron is ideal for this purpose because cast iron can take the considerable heat of the coals, plus it has a handle to protect your hands and convenient little legs to keep the hot bottom from burning the surface it's on, all while providing a smoldering surface to ignite your powdered incense and melt your resins.

And I tend to represent fire with, ya know, some fire! A lit candle, say. You'll find incense, candles, water, and salt alongside chalices, pentacles, swords, and wands on traditionally arranged altars, too, but I like to simplify where possible, especially because I practice alone and there's no one to compromise with—like, why represent earth with something else when I've got all of this earth right here under my feet, representing itself quite competently?

Once I've streamlined the process of representing the elements on my altar, I'm left with a surface that boasts a couple of cups, a candle, and an incense burner. There's nothing particularly Wiccan about that, although I found my way to these ritual habits through the Wiccan framework. This is a template that can lend itself to any ritual purpose on whatever magical path you invent for yourself. And of course, you're not limited to these items. The template is here for your embellishments. And flowers. You'll probably want some flowers.

Water, air, earth, fire. That's four, if you're counting. Spirit is the fifth element frequently represented on the altar, and that's where the shrine part comes in. Shrines differ from altars in that altars are considered a sacred workspace, while a shrine is considered a space dedicated to some entity, deity, or spirit concept of your choosing. A lot of altars include a shrine, so visually they tend to collapse into the same concept. Most religions have shrines, some physical representation of a nonphysical being to whom we pray or on whose example we meditate.

Everything's pretty straightforward except the spirit part. I'm almost reluctant to get into it. We were doing so well! We were all holding hands and singing, and no one was agnostic about the existence of water, earth, air, or fire. We weren't asking ourselves, "If earth really exists, why would it let mudslides happen to good people?" or "Why hath water forsaken me?" or consoling ourselves with the axiom "Air works in mysterious ways"—although it undoubtedly does. I guess I like to think of spirit or God/dess as a sort of composite character, one that combines the million and a half ways of being divine while allowing access to the individual deities that constitute the whole.

Bearing all that in mind makes it difficult for some of us to fully separate one goddess from another. For some witches and Pagans, worship of any god or goddess is worship of God/dess. In fact, studying the different forms that God/dess has taken across time and cultures is a big part of how a lot of folks practice. This massive divinity and its countless individual forms and faces is something that some of us need to honor just as surely as we do earth, air, fire, and water. But some of us don't. Some witches are agnostic. Some are philosophically skeptical, in that they believe only what they can verify, and they find plenty of value in their magical practice without the help of any of the myriad deities.

So what does spirit look like on the altar?

That's up to you. Any graven image will do, provided that it's spiritually resonant to you, and as long as it reminds you of an aspect of your best and most exalted self. A statue or 2-D image of a particular entity that inspires you could be nice. Maybe Prince or Albert Einstein if you're not into gods and goddesses. I might recommend staying away from living people because that's a little much. Make it *iconic*. Or if you're not into anthropomorphizing the divine (and I don't blame you), use your imagination to figure out how to fill this space in your template. Muslim and Jewish religious artists have been inventing ways to represent holiness without putting a face on it for millennia. Try your hand at it.

If you do decide to represent a deity on your altar, save room for offerings! The word "altar" actually means something like "a raised place for making offerings"; in ancient times this was generally a burnt offering of animal parts. Burnt, I imagine, to deliver the essence of the meat into the air so that it can rise to the heavens, where the gods hang out, huffing the fumes of devotion. Modern offerings are more often of the unburnt food and flowers varieties. The particular offering depends on what is sacred to the deity you choose. Get to googling! Researching god/desses and their personal preferences is so much fun. It reminds me of the research I did as a young tween to better obsess over a celebrity crush. If, for the sake of argument, my due diligence revealed that my heart-throb loved Twizzlers, the color yellow, and hiking in the forest, I could make an altar using yellow roses, pine incense, and a red licorice offering, so that they might smile upon me with favor. You get it? Do the same thing for the spirit that suits you, but perhaps don't make it a celebrity. That's weird! They're human.

Before moving on, I'll just mention that the traditional Wiccan altar has a few other items that I don't work with much at home, like the broom, or *besom*, which tends to be ornamental these days, but can be used to ritually sweep the air in a gesture of banishing bad vibes.

Another altar item is the *cauldron*, which you probably think of as the witch's cooking pot but was really anyone's cooking pot back in the day. The main purpose of the cauldron is as a vessel, a womb-shaped place for mixing elements together into something greater than the sum of its parts—whether that means cooking a lovely meal, mixing a potion, or using it as a heatproof container to transform candles, incense, or resin into the changes you want to see in the world. It's both a super-sturdy container and a pretty solid metaphor.

MAGICAL CHORES

My favorite thing to do with a cauldron is clean it. Indulge me! The first thing you do is scrape out whatever may have collected in it. If you use your cauldron for mixing/burning incense and resin, then you'll likely have a complicated-smelling collection of oily residues and ashes built up in there after a while. To get rid of all that junk, you cover the bottom of the cauldron with *Florida water* (or *agua florida*). Florida water is an American version of the French eau de Cologne, a light, unisex perfume water appropriate for use as an all-purpose toiletry item or, due to the properties of the floral extracts that give it its refreshing scent, a powerful and versatile spiritual cleansing agent for the body when applied to the skin, and for the home when added to a floor wash or used to wipe down altars and ritual items. Although it's certainly used secularly, it's popular (alongside holy water and various other flower waters) as a ritual cleansing item for people who practice Wicca, Santería, Hoodoo, and Voodoo. Of the many formulas out there, most Florida water blends contain a mixture of lavender, ber-gamot (sometimes neroli), lemon (sometimes orange), and cinnamon (sometimes clove). I'll talk more about some of the individual magical properties of each of these components in Chapter 4. So pour that Florida water in the cauldron, light a match, and toss the match in there. It makes a totally mesmerizing blue flame that will fill your cauldron like the Goblet of Fire. It's one of the more spectacular magic tricks I know, so try it! Impress your friends! Don't burn the house down! The Florida water will burn off in a minute, taking with it whatever residue was built up on your cauldron. It's also a very dramatic way to get rid of any little bits of magical refuse you might have: scraps of sigil paper, petition letters, tearstained poems, things you want to ritually shed. A good little cauldron fire, done safely, is an effective way for us apartment-dwelling witches to get things gone without too much trouble.

At the moment, my own dedicated altar space is sort of like a formal living room: it looks nice, but it's not really where I hang out. These days, I've been putting my magic—my faith, will, intentions, and actions—to the purpose of writing, so my altar-keeping practice has been applied to my workspace in such a way as to remind me of my goals. I've been working at my kitchen table, styling it to inspire and amuse me. One night I decided to use an old Ouija board as a desk blotter, and then I crowded the table with ferns (used magically to prevent evil from entering a home, although that's incidental—I just like ferns). They're potted in soil, obvs, so let's count that as earth. I burned a cool, refreshing green tea incense (air) to set a mood of relaxed focus. I'm sure I had any number of beverages before me (water), and in my grandma's old cast-iron candelabra I lit a trio of rainbow drip candles (fire). The candles are white, but somehow they drip multicolored wax. They are extremely magical. Presiding over this array, I placed the *Mona Lisa*, actual size, in a very fancy gilt frame. The moment I saw her at that yard sale, I knew we were meant to be together. Ms. Mona, Our Mother of Self-Possession, so serene and secure in the knowledge of something you don't know. That's the spirit!

So, you see, I did my best to make my immediate physical environment mirror the vision I'm trying to achieve—a chill, comfortable space to talk about mystical stuff without taking ourselves too seriously.

SUGGESTED READING

Amber K, *True Magick* (Llewellyn, 1990)

Janet and Stewart Farrar, *A Witches' Bible* (Phoenix Publishing, 1981)

Clarissa Pinkola Estes, *Women Who Run with the Wolves* (Ballantine Books, 1992)

Chapter 2

ROY G. BIV DEVOE, OR COLORS

Now that you know where to do your magic, let's look at the elements that you can think about when constructing spells.

Color magic is fascinating because it's some of the most quotidian magic around. Anytime color is imbued with emotion or made to carry some meaning beyond the literal, a certain measure of color magic is being performed. I'm using the term "magic" to mean some transformation of intention or belief (in the form of thought) into some tangible result—red reminds you of sex, you wear a red dress with that intention, you go out in it, and you are sexy. You just did some red magic. It's so simple I feel stupid writing it down. I mean, there's an emoji for this phenomenon. 💃

You saw it in a movie and on TV and in a book and heard it from some sax-heavy rock ballad, but maybe you didn't really think of that as magic even though the guy in the song said "Oh oh it's magic" or "Everything she does is magic, magic,

magic." Maybe you thought magic was something other than making your ideas real.

Colors are essential signifiers to consider when building a spell. A lot of magical work is about setting the mood that matches your intention, and in the context of spellbuilding, colors are like physical manifestations of a mood. We have a lot of choices of color, and therefore a broad range of color-bound associations to bring to the party. And it *is* a party, because I'm about to spin the color wheel like a game of Twister and explain those color associations as we use them where I'm from. I will also continue to make really stupid puns and port-manteaus, like I did there in the chapter title. See, I combined Roy G. Biv, the mnemonic device for the colors of the rainbow that some of us learned in school, with the last part of the name of an R&B group from my youth called Bell Biv DeVoe, and poof—just like magic, it was hilarious and we all laughed.

Schticky dad humor is a big part of the witchy culture I'm steeped in, and I wouldn't want you to miss out on all of the semantic fun.

The short story about the colors is as follows:

- Red: Mars, motivation, fire, sexual attraction
- Orange: Mercury, communication, success
- Yellow: sun, attraction, joy
  - Green: Venus, money, abundance, luck
  - Blue: peace, protection, relaxation
  - Indigo: ugh, there is no indigo in this system. I never should have brought Roy G. into this.
- Violet, aka purple, aka purps: recognition, expansion, wisdom

There are black, white, pink, gold, and brown as well. Consider those the DeVoe in this scenario. See? It's funny. We're laughing. We're enjoying ourselves. And we should be, because this part's not rocket science.

But before we discuss the magical properties of colors, I'd like to take a sec to appreciate the totally scientific magic of how we're able to perceive color in the first place. Let's do a little research on the human eye's ability to perceive color. And by research, I mean let's try to string together the ten or twelve things about the human eye's ability that I've gleaned here and there, like a greasy-fingered little grifter, from public radio, Maggie Nelson books, and playing an old favorite game my friends and I call Science or Bullshit. You can intuit the rules, I'm sure, but it involves telling your friends something incredible about the natural world and universe that you heard somewhere but you don't remember where.

It's a well-known science fact that eyeballs are weird gooey spheres with an iris that acts like a little camera shutter, opening and closing, to let in the appropriate amount of light as it bounces off the objects that surround us. White light contains a full spectrum of color, as becomes apparent when you bend the white light through a prism, producing that sweet Roy G. Biv DeVoe rainbow effect that we all find so pleasing. What we're really noticing when we perceive an item's color, like the greenness of grass, is the result of the chemicals in the grass (most prominently chlorophyll) absorbing all of the colors of the light *except* for the green part. It rejects the green part of the spectrum and reflects it back. There's a saying, taught to me by my uncle Bill (Nye the Science Guy), that goes: We don't see things, we see light reflecting off things.

But receiving reflected light off objects through the iris is only the first step in the seeing process. The lens of the eye changes shape to bring the blurry mess of light into quick focus and beams it over to the retina, the photosensitive inner layer of the eye, which acts like the film in a camera by capturing an impression of the image and relaying it through the optic nerve to the brain. The brain does the trick of assembling all this stimuli into some recognizable shape, the next page of the flip book. In fact, my uncle Bill tells me that some scientists think of the eyes and the optic nerve system as *parts of the brain*, at which I rejoice! I like the notion that the eyes are organs of interpretation in their own right, not just a couple of impartial cameras administering a live feed to your rational mind. Your eyes are a mind of their own. Barely a page into this rough exploration and all that pure visual data we assume we've been processing diligently and scientifically is sullied by our treacherous mind's interpretive dance.

So how do we make any sense of the shimmering mess of the world? I guess that's the magic question. We start by making distinctions, creating categories into which to sort things, color-coded for your mental organization. What follows is a rough guide to some commonly held magical color associations and a few of the endless variations in which they can be employed for witchy purposes.

RED

Red is our business today, and red would be really mad at me for getting distracted by science from the charge-forward head butt of its energy. Red is the beacon meant to physiologically arrest you *now*, hence the cue of the stop sign hue. Red demands attention. It signals sweetness, ripeness, or poison. Your pick, but choose quickly, because red is nothing if not

The Seattle Public Library
Columbia Branch
www.spl.org

Checked Out On: 12/5/2023 16:03
XXXXXXXXX2845

Item Title	Due Date
0010095115704	12/26/2023
Enchantments : a modern witch's guide to self-possession	
0010102758942	12/26/2023
Learn to code by solving problems : a Python programming primer	

# of Items: 2

Renew items at www.spl.org/MyAccount
or 206-386-4190
Sign up for due date reminders
at www.spl.org/notifications

ind your next read with curated picks
m our staff! www.spl.org/StaffPicks

decisive. Red is about sex, or more aptly, the friction parts of sex. I like to think of red lipstick as the foundational, "sexy lady"–type magic of the late capitalist era. While it's one of those quotidian spells that feminine people cast ten times a day without acknowledging it as such, rouging one's lips is a powerful reminder: first you and then everyone else who sees your upper mouth will be subtly, subconsciously reminded of your nether mouth, should you be so lucky as to have one. I'm talking about your vulva! And so will everyone else be if you keep it up with all this red color magic. The soles of the most expensive and status-symbol-y shoes, Louboutins, are a vivid bloody red for a reason. There's no way that they would hold the same covetous fascination if they were lavender on the underside. And consider for a moment, as I'm sure Nathaniel Hawthorne did, that a cerulean letter could never quite convey the same slut-shaming power that a scarlet one would.

Every living being is some sort of sexual consequence. That's some powerful fucking energy to make so much happen, to turn so many impulses into realities. And birth and sex are as red as it gets. Red's the first color humans painted and adorned themselves with. It has the shortest wavelength, meaning that it wins the race to your brain via your eyeballs over the other colors. Red represents the instinctual drives that keep us eating, fucking, and fighting our way into the future. Red is the impetus, the impetuousness, the fricative heat of transformation, the generative blood of the uterus, the pulp that becomes us.

Any yogis in the house will know that the chakra system originates in the Upanishads, the ancient living texts that, combined with the Vedas, inform Hinduism and the practice of yoga. The Sanskrit word *chakra* literally means "wheel," but it's used to describe areas of the body that act as gathering centers for different types of energy.

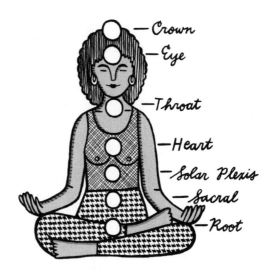

Red is associated with the root, or *muladhara*, chakra, which is the foundation or basis of physical nature and of our sense of safety and security. (I'm hedging a little as I say that, since the systems don't align exactly, they overlap, so I find it helpful to mention them alongside each other.) The muladhara chakra is associated with the organs of reproduction, elimination, and, uncoincidentally, the pelvic floor, the essential band of muscle that serves to keep all your insides from falling out your ass. I'd say that's pretty foundational. And red.

What Are You Gonna Do About It?
The Sanskrit character for the muladhara chakra is one that we might carve on a red candle for someone who wants to feel a deeper sense of grounding in the world, or to help someone

recommit to practicing self-care when it comes to eating, sleeping, and hydrating properly—ya know, the basics that keep us feeling firmly rooted. Red is the color of my girl Nette's (see also "Let's Play 'Nette or Nettle?'" in Chapter 4) now infamous potion Filthy Sheets, the illest sexual attraction formula around. If a smell could be said to be "guttural," this would be a guttural smell. If "groin-y" was a word, I would use it to describe this formula. It promises a strictly carnal effect. It is not meant to inspire any fluffy lovey feelings whatsoever; it's just a powerful below-the-belt hit. Some TV writer got a bottle and it had such a dramatic effect (from zero to banging a bartender in the bathroom within hours!) that they passed it around the writers' room to unanimous reports of leg humpery and polyamorous invitations. It was only a couple of months before it was featured in their show as pivotal exonerating evidence in a fictional murder trial, spurring the adorable little rhyme "If the sheets are filthy, then she is not guilty."

I did a red spell recently in solidarity with International Women's Day that included a red female figure candle, which is kinda like a Barbie-sized wax model. People would typically use this candle in a spell to either (a) attract an enthusiastically amorous lady or (b) themselves become said enthusiastically amorous lady in an attractive sort of way. I'm all for those purposes, but that day I lit mine in solidarity with women around the world who wore red to bring awareness to women's rights and, in particular, in protest against the actions and policies of our misogynist president. I placed the candle on my altar (this time the altar was in my bathtub) along with a red rubber ball and a bottle of glue arranged in a triangle, because a triangle looked cool. I played "I'm Every Woman" real loud and sang along with it. The lyrics are perfect for identifying yourself with an omnipotent goddess figure, while grounding that power in the possession of all women and femmes. But if you're not into Ashford and Simpson, Chaka, or Whitney (for shame), then try Nikki Giovanni's poem "Ego Trippin (there may be a reason why)," or any song that makes you feel bad AF in a ladylike sorta way.

You're probably starting to get the picture: be every woman—the intention is represented by the candle. The red rubber ball was something I found serendipitously around the house, which sent me searching for the glue, because it reminded me of the most ancient, powerful, and juvenile reversing spell: "I'm rubber, you're glue." Folks were calling for witches to straight-up hex the Trump administration, and I understand the inclination. That administration is heinous. I'm so not into hexing, though. It's a bad, bad look. The furthest I would go in that direction is this reversing spell. I prefer a "don't start nothing, won't be nothing" approach.

PINK

Pink magic is a variation on red magic, obvs. These aren't exactly secret esoteric associations. They're totally normal human associations that we all take part in constructing and reinforcing. We give these colors power with our belief and shared experience of them. Colors transcend our individuality and allow us access to a commonality of experience, a shared lexicon. Across many cultures we think of pinkness and cuteness in the same space. We associate pink with affection, with the flirtation of spring and cherry blossoms. It's held sacred to Venus, Aphrodite, Erzulie (a Haitian *loa*, or goddess of African origin), and other love goddesses who, despite bearing differ-ent names and origins, perform a similar function of crystal-lizing an ideal of romantic love in feminine form. The goddess comes in as many forms and guises as the world makes neces-sary, but often she takes as sacred to her the color pink because it is the blush of health, the manifestation of the blood closest to the skin. The desire for intimacy that, instead of the urgent demand and friction of red, brings a cute doodling-hearts-in-your-notebook kind of sensation.

Some Uses for Pink Things

Pink candles, incense, and potions are used for romantic love magic: to attract a new love situation, deepen an existing one, or heal/uncross from a love situation that didn't work out. I think it's an important and often overlooked point that the same sort of magic romantic crush energy that some of us produce in excess and project in weird directions (you know who you are) can be turned inward. Applying that sort of affection to yourself, fixating and rhapsodizing on your best and most adorable qualities by the light of a pink candle, sounds like a pretty excellent love attraction spell to me. It's easier to appreciate someone when you have an idea of how it's done.

MYSTIC CRYSTAL RAINBOWS

A handy rule of thumb when it comes to crys-tals is that you can usually tell what a stone can be most helpful with by its color. You're starting to understand the magical associations of color; generally speaking, the same logic carries over to the uses of crystals, gems, and stones. So it shouldn't surprise you that pink stones can be used in conjunction with love magic. For example, people use rose quartz to tune in to its vibration of unconditional love for oneself and others. Pink tourmaline is worn or carried to attract friendly platonic love, possibly due to its reputation in stone lore for increasing one's capacity for sympathy toward other people. Watermelon tourmaline is a pale red tourmaline encased within a sort of "rind" of green tourmaline, representing a balance between projecting and receptive energies—the kind of balance that witchy people seek within themselves and in relationship with a partner.

ORANGE

Orange magic is for success, the transformation of your will into the physical manifestation of your goal. It's the color of the solar plexus, the seat of creative energy in the body. Orange (and copper, but let's just call it all orange for now) is associated with Mercury, and mercurial magic is associated with language, commerce, and the energetic spark between people that is facilitated through conversation and exchange of information. Orange represents the turning point when potential energy is transformed into kinetic energy. Did you ever hear that thing about painting your kitchen or dining room orange because it's supposed to stimulate the appetite? Orange is that kindling color.

What's It For?

A witch who felt stuck in a rut creatively or professionally might choose to carve an orange candle to focus on being open to recognizing a spark of inspiration, or to aid in a job-hunting spell that connects to the mercurial vibes of eloquence and wit (for conducting smooth interviews) and bestows a propensity to be in the right place at the right time (for serendipitous networking). The formulas for success and Mercury and lucky job potions are all blends of essential oils and herbs you can use for focusing your energy toward getting a new gig, and all call for a rusty, orangeish, coppery color to link them to the various deities of communication and inspiration (especially when it comes to the written or spoken word), a great many of whom also take orange as their sacred signature color. This association feels right to me because copper is a particularly conductive metal. It carries electrons with great agility. That's why it's used for the electrical wiring that operates within our communication devices. People who make wands and magical jewelry tend to use copper wire to bind the elements together for the same reason—copper is thought to be similarly conductive of energy in the *witchier* sense of the term.

Copper can be useful in love magic, again for its conductive, connective, pliable quality. It is associated with the love goddess Oshun, whom we'll talk more about in a minute. Her altar often features offerings of copper pennies in multiples of five. Copper is also sacred to Venus and her little buddy Cupid. You can think of your copper jewelry as devoted to these deities, magnetically attracting the love attention you want. Connecting your intention to an item to be worn is what people refer to as creating a *talisman*, and copper is one of the preferred metals for the job.

YELLOW AND GOLD

I'm eager to get around to yellow and gold because I can't wait to talk about the sun and its heat and the sexy way light has of being both particle and ray. I love bothness—so much magic is possible when things defy their category, when we refuse to stay put or keep a single shape. When we do yellow magic we're tapping into the solar type of energy that you'll know from the joy of the warmth of the sun, the spotlight, the pleasure of being seen. Glory.

Sunlight purifies, and yellow is often a component color in healing spells. A healing incense blend I'm familiar with is bright and fluffy with golden life-everlasting blossoms, which have been smoked medicinally in the Americas to relieve headaches. In fact, a great many healing herbs and flowers associated magically with the sun are bright and yellow, like chamomile and calendula, and used for soothing and disinfecting.

Que Más?

Yellow is also used magically as a way to invite and inspire a solar type of brightness to a situation. At the shop we make Solar Blast candles for people's birthdays, as a birthday is the anniversary of the sun's return (more or less) to the position it was in when you were born.

Anything Else?

If you want to do a spell to find something in particular, that's called, very generally, attraction magic. I tend to use yellow attraction magic in apartment-hunting spells. I can't give away the seals and sigils we use at Enchantments to you guys for free, but I can tell you that you wouldn't be totally crazy to carve or draw a simple symbol of a house to indicate a home, arrows drawing inward, and some symbol of the sun (hint: it'll probably look like a sun). You can also use solar magic via gold or yellow to highlight an aspect of yourself if you're trying to stand out from the crowd in, say, an audition situation. When you're hoping to achieve nearly any form of distinction or swaggery, gold and yellow may effectively be used for the purposes of dabbin' on them fools.

GREEN

There are so many ways of looking at the color green that I'm not sure where to start. One place could be the heart chakra. By now, we know that chakras are energy centers in the body (the subtle, internal, invisible body). The heart chakra is called *anahata* or "unstruck," as if to imply that inside an open, compassionate heart is a place that may remain miraculously invulnerable to destruction. This chakra is the seat, perhaps unsurprisingly, of the emotional being, and is associated with the color green. The color green and the heart chakra are in turn associated with Lakshmi, Hindu goddess of love and abundance. The distinction between money and abundance is often neglected. In a Venn diagram they definitely overlap, but abundance is a much more comprehensive concept. Money is like an effigy of abundance, a stunt dummy. But with Lakshmi, the heart chakra, and the color green, we're talking about the real thing—abundance of family, friends, food, opportunity. And yes, money too.

Things to Try

Green candles are commonly used for money magic, even in places that don't have green money. Dollar signs, arrows, and that creepy eye-of-Sauron pyramid are the sorts of images you might intentionally inscribe on green candles, your wallet, your waitress apron, and so on if you want to boost your cash flow. We'll talk more about money drawing later (see Chapter 10), but it's a very green department.

More Things to Try

Another form of green magic, one many people will think of first, is the magic of herbs, plants, trees, and flowers (see Chapter 4, on plants and minerals, for much more in this realm). "Green magic" is a general term that, at least to me, refers to all variety of herbalism, rootwork, and agriculture. Folk knowledge of healing plants—how best to cultivate and harvest them, and how to understand and employ their power—is the foundation of nearly all of our modern magical practices. In Wicca, the basis of observance is a close attentiveness to the natural world, a desire to live our lives in harmony with nature, and recognition of the divinity in all living things. One of the most useful magic books I know of is *Cunningham's Encyclopedia of Magical Herbs.* It's a reference book of plants, beautifully illustrated, with engagingly detailed descriptions of their origins and traditional magical uses. It's a great entry point for anyone interested in finding out more about the green magic of plant life.

BLUE

I love the boundlessness of blue; it feels more ethereal than other colors. The sky, the sea, and the night itself all challenge our minds and eyes to try to wrap themselves around their immensity. It eludes me in my efforts to capture it. It makes me stretch for all my five-dollar words but still I come up with a handful of air. There's pleasure in the stretch.

But for real, though, I'm not gonna scat a bunch of word-jazz all over the color blue. I'm just going to tell you . . .

How It's Used in Magic

Blue is for peace and protection intentions, like for house bless-ing. When moving into a new place, or trying to clear the air between roommates, burning a blue house-blessing candle is the thing to do because its coolness of tone is meant to lend itself to harmonious relations, lack of conflict, and peaceful-ness. This sort of neutralizing and protecting intention is often considered lunar magic, and moons are commonly found in house-blessing symbols; the moon hanging above a home as a beacon or sentinel, keeping watch, could be a useful image to conjure up in whatever your house-blessing style might be. Note the moon we hang outside of the store.

That's Not All

For more portable protection, there are a few books on psy-chic (in the sense of being non-physical in its application) self-defense that we suggest to people at the store, but I'll give you the gist of what I found most useful—which is what Nette told me when I said I didn't want to read the book and would she please just give me the gist of what I would find useful and she did, bless her black metal heart. The trick to this method of psychic self-defense (and my research has revealed a few other magical people who recommend the same tech-nique) is to visualize oneself inside a blue bubble, not at all unlike a giant Advil gelcap. That's how Nette does hers, at least. Mine is more like a full-body condom, a deflector shield kind of like the starship *Enterprise* has, and it's blue. Atop it all, above my head, is a/the light source. In my case, that's often literally the light fixture in the subway car, 'cause I usually do this meditation on the train as a way to ground myself and make a clear psychic boundary between me and anything or anyone that's not serving me, and also as a way to appropriate a little personal space in one of the most public environments. I uncross my legs, plant my feet on the floor and let myself feel like they're rooted there, then pay attention to each area of my body as I scan upward and sort of inspect and imagine this shield around me. By the time I get up to my head I re-imagine the light source above me as the sun, a giant glam disco ball, a freaking Edison lightbulb, whatever. My posture aligns, and I'm left feeling confident and radiant and purposeful. The cool part is that when I'm faced with a moment that's likely to cause alarm and be triggering, I can find myself inside my bubble observing the stress roll off like rain on glass. It's beautiful to witness myself protected, with the confidence to move forward, in control of my actions and my reactions— someone who's not being puppeted by the negativity of others. Anyway, the bubble is blue, and it's blue for a reason, the same as Glinda the Good Witch's bubble, and you too can have such a shield. See, I said I'd give you real, concrete examples and then I told you to do something totally imaginary and weird in public. I'm impossible.

PURPLE

As Shug Avery once said, via Alice Walker, I think it pisses God off if you walk by the color purple in a field somewhere and don't notice it. Shug knows exactly what's up. I'm not one to adhere too firmly to a particular sect or mode of worship, but if pressed I could accurately be described as a Shug Averite. Her opinions on God suit me just fine, but she's particularly on point with purple, as suggested by the book's title. Purple is used magically for recognition, as a symbol of nobility and greatness. Existing as it does at the end of the spectrum visible to the human eye, it is also used to represent or evoke an elevated spiritual consciousness.

Purple is associated with the third-eye chakra, located in the pineal gland slightly above and behind the eyes. The pineal gland is primarily responsible for producing melatonin, the chemical that governs sleep cycles. Biologically, the pineal gland has the attributes of a light-sensitive organ, although it doesn't receive light directly, being positioned as it is *inside your face*. Still, it produces melatonin at varying levels depending on the amount of light information it receives, which explains it being referred to as an inner eye. It's thought of by many yogis, spiritualists, and woo-woo people of all stripes as the point of connection/overlap between the mind (individual consciousness) and the divine (universal consciousness). In this context a lot of witchy folks use purple for meditation, contemplation of the "higher mysteries," and thinking super-groovy mystic thoughts.

What Does This Practice Actually Look Like?

It could be as simple as meditating on the color purple—just breathing and being still and thinking, if of anything at all, of purple. Or it could be as complicated as an elaborately conducted hallucinogenic journey . . . with strangers . . . in a loft. Some witches use purple (oils, incense, stones, etc.) to encourage psychic awareness, receiving visions or a divine inspiration of visionary ideas.

Of Jupes and Purps

Purple is also associated with the planet Jupiter (see more in Chapter 5), and in that regard it's used for spells of growth and expansion, gaining recognition from authority, advancement within an order or within a hierarchy, or gaining recognition from your peers. I carved a purple candle for a lady who had done everything she needed to do to get a promotion at work—she earned it, first of all. Then she found the strength to ask for what she wanted, went through negotiations, and got everyone to sign off, but still they were stringing her along, saying that they were waiting for funding to come through. She wanted something to help her move up and/or out of her position, to wherever she needed to be to have her talents recognized. Amen, honey.

BROWN

Brown is associated with the Earth, capital *E*, because of earth, lowercase *e*. It's the soil, in its fertile mystery, in its shitty fecundity. And maybe because of that, maybe because all of us who are alive succumb to the humus eventually, in some magical systems brown represents justice—not in the

context of human laws, which are so changeable and so arbi-
trarily enforced as to miss the mark of actual justice, but in
the ideal sense of the great leveler, the equalizing notion of
the grave, the sense of collectivity that is the root of true
justice—that is, we're all in the same boat here on planet
Earth, and the brown facts are that we live our lives wrapped
up in our brown fallible flesh, we depend on the brown fertility of the earth for food, we depend on brown decaying matter
to keep that soil alive and able to sustain life. We all do. Brown
is keeping you and me alive and fruitful while we might not
even notice, because brown is the energy that does what needs
to be done on this earthly plane and doesn't make a big fucking deal about it. Every one of us shits, bleeds, and sheds hair
and cells, brownly. In recognizing, honoring, and having
gratitude for this process, one may become grounded, which
is one of the most useful purposes of brown magic. Oh yeah,
and I'm pretty sure it's the only way to be happy in life at all,
BTW. Just saying.

Getting and staying grounded isn't easy for some of us.
What are you supposed to do? Put your hands and feet in the
dirt? Eat breakfast every day? Go hiking? Bake your own
bread? If you figure it out, let me know.

BLACK

Next is black magic, *so spoooooky*. Oh my God, stop. You're
freaking me out. People in the store get all weird about just
seeing or touching the black candles sometimes. It's funny.
The people who profess to have not the least belief in magic
seem to be the most fervent believers in the evil, destructive
force of what amounts to an XXL black crayon with a wick in

it. They're still just made of wax, you guys. Wax that was dyed and poured into a mold in a factory in Brooklyn that is called, ironically, Crusader—ironic given that the Crusades were purportedly about the urgent necessity of everybody in the whole world, or at least everybody in the world that those ignoramuses knew of, to worship the same god in the same way, and now those Crusader candles are used primarily for Pagan purposes. Imagine the sound of cackling laughter.

As we might intuit from our little science lesson earlier, black absorbs the full spectrum of light and reflects nothing back, so magical logic follows that black would absorb and neutralize other energies. In its vastness, black is associated with the outer limits, the unknown, and death, the fear and avoidance of which is one of humanity's most persistent limitations.

But yeah, everyone seems to have an idea about black magic. Even people who know nothing else know with certainty that witches use black candles for evil. I mean it's true, sure. Some witches do use black candles to hone and further their bad intentions and to use their personal strength and energy to manipulate and wish harm on other people. I hate to be the bearer of bad news, but some people are, sadly, just assholes. And some of those assholes are witches. Some people will use any little filament of power they have or find for the purpose of hurting other people. People will use their physical power, their power to manipulate, or their power to withdraw—anything handy, really—in a misguided effort to make themselves feel whole. Witchy people are no different. Some people use black color magic to concentrate their negativity for their own cruel intentions, à la all the horror movies with witches in them. But if you know what you're doing, you can certainly use black candles and implements for constructive purposes.

Examples, You Say? Well, I'll Tell Ya

Black is associated with Saturn, the teacher of the real-ass lessons that one might prefer to avoid. Saturn was the most distant observable planet in the time before telescopes, and therefore it came to represent the outer limits, the edge of the universe as far as folks knew (more on this in Chapter 5). So black is used for setting boundaries. Very useful and non-evil black spells can be done with the help of master oil, an old Hoodoo formula (recipes vary) you can use as an aid to willpower and discipline, to setting limits for yourself; master oil would be a potential component in a weight loss spell, in order to inspire commitment to new routines.

If you'd like another perfectly moral black spell that you can do for yourself with a minimum of fuss, hellfire, and eternal damnation, my fave is Don't Play Yourself, a spell of my own devising. You'll need to get your hands on:

- A hand mirror with a black frame, nothing fancy (try the dollar store)
- Permanent black marker
- Letter stencil (cheap plastic, like the kind a kid might have for school)

Take your time with the mirror and the stencil and your hands to spell out this essential, timeless reminder on the surface: DON'T PLAY YOURSELF. Mine looks like this:

Concentrate, don't fuck it up! JK, you can always use rubbing alcohol to make corrections. Since a magic mirror is involved here, the use it's to be put to is technically called *scrying*, a form of divination that involves abstracted, meditative gazing into some sort of reflective surface while taking note of and interpreting the ideas that come to you in the process. The purpose of this spell is to contact the part of yourself that knows better than to sad-sack around after someone who's just not checking for you at all, the part of yourself that knows better than to let you be underestimated, undervalued, or misused by anyone. That boundary starts in your relationship with you. Use this mirror when you need reminding.

WHITE/GRAY/SILVER

White Is for Witching

You can use white for any magical intention. Just like white light contains all the colors, all intentions can be furthered through white, if that's all you've got or that's all you want to use. You can do money magic on white, house blessing on white, fertility on white. Really, anything. But beyond its all-purpose capacity, white is used more particularly for cleansing, healing, and uncrossing. It's associated with spiritual purity, physical health, and sanity. I know that you already know this because the association of white with purity and rebirth is shared among Muslims, Jews, Christians, Wiccans, practitioners of Santería and Voodoo, Sikhs, Hindus, Buddhists, and Zoroastrians. Miraculously, we hold this in common. It's the color of the initiate or novice, representing the blank slate.

White is associated with the moon, cool, dreamy, and ethereal. Silver is lunar as well, used for protective magic, and for getting into that lunar feminine vibe, the mysterious nature of one who's always changing, continuously in flux. Gray is used for lunar spells of balancing and neutralizing erratic energies, as the color gray is the result of a tempering of the white and the black.

Okay! We've made it to the other side of the rainbow! Hopefully we've established a few things, first being that magic practice makes use of the associations we are already familiar with, but it uses them to achieve an intention. And second, that the colors and the concepts wrapped up in them are essential elements (read: choices you need to make) in magic and ritual. I've offered only a few of the countless potential uses of color in ritual, but now, if I did my job, you'll know a bit better what you're looking for when you do further experimentation and research. Go boldly.

Chapter 3

WAX WORK, OR CANDLES

The custom-carved intention candle is our bread and butter at Enchantments. We've made them in basically the same manner since 1982, although some of the seals, oils, and best practices have evolved over time. You don't need an Enchantments witch to enchant a candle, though. Don't tell people I said that, but it's true. All you need is one very particular and well-considered intention, a symbol that condenses your intention into an image, and a candle of the color and size that match your intention. Anointing oils, handmade incense, iron filings, honey, crushed herbs, and glitter are welcome and common additions, but they are not strictly necessary for an effective candle spell. You want to make one, don't you? Of course you do! It's a lovely way to focus your intentions and make them real. And it's a particularly useful tool for demonstrating how to combine all the different magical elements we've been talking about in one place. Let's go.

STEP 1: THE INTENTION

Before we get ahead of ourselves, we need to address the most important part of your spell candle: the intention behind it. What do you want to use this lovely focus tool to focus on? This has to be the first question because it's the hardest one to answer. Spend some time visualizing the desired outcome of your intention. If too many intentions come to mind at once and you have a hard time choosing, Enchantments witches tend to recommend an uncrossing candle—a powerful clearance of any blockages or confusion. If nothing at all comes to mind, I recommend a devotional candle, or something to express gratitude for what you have. The only thing you can't have enough of is gratitude, right? Let's use a full-moon gratitude candle as our example going forward.

ENCHANTED ORIGINS

Back in the 1970s, a couple of witchy weirdos, Herman Slater and Eddie Buczynski, opened up a place called The Magickal Childe, a little Chelsea storefront that sold strange old books and talismanic junk and served as a hub for the city's ever-growing population of magickal children, harbored several interweaving covens, and, oh my God and Goddess, spawned a great deal of gossip, intrigue, and magickal drama among said magickal children.

Bull of Heaven is a very thorough biography of the store's originators that tells the story of the evolution of modes and styles in the magical life of NYC, and it goes into *a lot* of detail about the push and pull of different ingroups and out-groups, the ontological differences between those groups, and the splintering and reformation of different covens and organizations during a wave of reinvigorated interest in Pagan spirituality.

Back then a lot of witches were still practicing their spirituality in secret, skyclad (in the nude) in their suburban backyards, and although he was devoted, scholarly, and charismatic by all accounts, Eddie was never able to achieve the authority from his high priest and priestess to hive-off, or start his own coven. It's possible that they did not want their tradition to be associated with a bunch of loudmouthed gays from the city with a giant neon pentagram in their storefront window. But who can really say? This rejection inspired him to create new spaces, covens, and rituals that would bear some things in common with the Gardnerian style of Wicca but make room for people of color and homos who at the time lacked access to those witchy traditions as a matter of course.

So The Magickal Childe came to be a sort of shop-cum-clubhouse for those magically inclined cape-wearing freakazoids. (Fun fact! Witches love capes! All of us do. Ask anyone!) A few of the employees there developed the style of candle carving and decoration that we use at Enchantments today, although the seals, oils, and best practices have evolved over time.

STEP 2: CHOOSE YOUR CANDLE

Does size matter? The answer, as in all magical things, is: Yes. No. Sometimes. When asking yourself what size candle to use for your purpose, the question isn't how powerful you want your spell to be but how long you plan to work on it. The strength of the spell is proportional to the strength of your will, not the size of your tools. You'll want to determine the length of time you're aiming to center your will on this particular goal and choose accordingly. If you use a big seven-day candle in glass and you don't put it out, it'll burn for about a week, hence the name. This can be a particularly useful feature for people who like to time their candle spells to the phase of the moon, because one week is a full quarter of the lunar cycle. When I choose to time a spell to the moon phase, I follow the logic that if my intention is to manifest something or if I want to see some element of life increase or grow, I would do it during the first half of the cycle, while the moon is waxing (getting bigger on the way to full), thus enlisting the moon as another reminder of my intention growing toward its fulfillment. If there's some element of life that needs to be released or diminished in importance, I might time that spell to the waning moon, so that in addition to watching my candle burn down to nothing, I get to see the moon whittled down to darkness, adding another layer of resonance to my intention. That's why the candle spell is so fun and effective. It's an able container for layers of resonance. Another reason that people like to use a seven-day candle for magic is that it shines its light on the days sacred to the sun, moon, Mars, Mercury, Jupiter, Venus, and Saturn. The whole gang! Well, not quite, but it's a nice assortment. Most mystical traditions assign significance to the days of the week, so the same seven-days-covers-all-bases logic can carry over to whatever you're working with.

But what if you have something more immediate in mind? Your intention won't be completely released until the candle is completely burned, so you might be better off with a candle that burns completely in an evening—a votive or dinner taper size. Whatever size you go with, fire safety is a concern! I've mentioned before how important it is to only burn candles on clutter-free surfaces and away from flammable stuff. If you're not comfortable leaving a larger candle burning in your house when you're not there, you have a few options. First, you can just put it out. Light it back up when you're ready. It'll take longer to burn this way, but so what? At least you won't be worried about it. Alternatively, you can put it in the sink or the bathtub when you're out so that it's contained and clear of anything flammable.

In candle magic, as in all things, the best, most powerful tools are the ones you actually have access to, so don't drive yourself crazy looking for pure beeswax dyed with natural berries, or assume that you can't do a candle spell unless you have access to an occult shop that sells them. Use what you've got, or what you can find semi-serendipitously in your neighborhood. My corner store carries candles in glass in a bunch of colors, both with and without images of the BVM and the baby Jesus printed on the sides. Just the other day I found the most magical rainbow-colored one at the deli where I was getting a sandwich (provolone, lettuce, tomato, jalapeño, oil, vinegar, and mustard on a hero). I know that I live in the greatest city in the world, but you can almost certainly find something serviceable at your grocery or dollar store: yahrzeit, shabbat, Chanukah, tea light, votive, taper, birthday, whatever. I'm reminded of a mystical scene in Neil Gaiman's *Anansi Boys* in which magical practitioners find themselves improvising some epically powerful magic with "black tapers" that were, in reality, oddly scented and decoratively shaped like penguins, while saying their incantations over a cauldron full of "mixed herbs" spice mix from the back of the cupboard. You know that platitude about gift-giving—it's the thought that counts? And how it's kinda bullshit? Well, in magic it's actually true! Your honed attention and intention are what really count. We choose the rest of this stuff—the candles, colors, scents, et cetera—as a way of building a support system around your intention to help it grow into fruition. I think I'm describing a garden lattice now, for all of you keeping score at home. Back to our imagined moon candle.

Let's do a seven-day spell. I'm gonna make it on a lunar white candle (see Chapter 2), but someone else might want to make it gray or silver or even blue. Witch's choice! Truly, your intentions are the star of the show here. It's just that the candle is physical, tangible, and on fire, so it's a little bit more immediate to the senses than the idea of your intention is. The work of a candle spell is to figure out how to metaphorically or metaphysically cram that intention into the candle in the form of the elements we've already talked about, like color and size, and now through symbols.

STEP 3: CHOOSE YOUR SYMBOLS

We're doing something lunar, so moon shapes will work nicely for our symbols. Make up your own design or get ye to image searching. We'll talk more about making your own sigils at the end of this chapter, but for now I think this triple goddess symbol will work for us:

It's used by neo-Pagans to represent the goddess in her three phases; maiden (waxing moon: inception), mother (full moon: fulfillment), and crone (waxing moon: repose). "Every woman, and every goddess-form contain all three—both cyclically and simultaneously," according to Janet and Stewart Farrar, authors of *A Witches' Bible* and a good portion of the modern Wiccan canon. But don't let this metaphor of female biology limit the usefulness of the symbolism. It can be for everybody, regardless of the condition of their physical body. Let's put it on the candle!

How, though? If your candle isn't trapped inside a glass, you can pop it out and carve your symbol into its surface. At the store we carve the symbols into the wax with a dulled knife or carving tool, and they come out looking pretty rad, but it takes practice. In the end, it's your time, thought, and energy that make it worth a damn. Put your back into it! If you can't get the candle out of its container, you can simply draw your symbol on the glass with a permanent marker.

STEP 4: THE ANOINTING

"Anointing" is a very foreboding word for greasing up or, like, lotioning. It's also known as dressing the candle with an oil that matches your purpose. This would be a good time to check your witches' herbal (or your witches' internet) to find out which plant extracts and scents go along with what you're working on (see more in Chapter 4). Luckily for us, our spell is for the moon, and I happen to have some coconut oil in my kitchen, which, according to *Cunningham's Encyclopedia*, is sacred to lunar deities. Coco it is. Olive oil is another one to try if you don't have access to more fragrant options. Take a teaspoon or so of your oil, less for a small candle, and rub it into all the nooks and crannies you carved. Then take some glitter or a colorful powder of crushed herbs or dried flower petals (check which are safe to burn) and work them into the sticky grooves of your design. I chose silver glitter for my imaginary lunar candle, but you might use pulverized lavender blossoms or something. No matter. If you drew your sigil on the glass, you can just add a few drops of oil to the top of the candle, and a sprinkle of glitter if you like. What you're left with is something like this. I think it looks great:

MAKE A PIN CANDLEHOLDER

If you don't have a candleholder to fit the candle you're about to burn, you can make one really easily. Take a lid from a jar and stick a thumb tack into it from the top, piercing the lid all the way through. Turn the lid over and you have a handy little spike to stick the end of your candle on and a clever little dish to catch the melted wax.

STEP 5: PREPARE THE GLASS

(If your candle doesn't have a glass, that's fine. Arrange any combo of the following items on your altar, or near your candle.)

Some candle magicians like to use the candle glass to hold even more magical material that you can layer into your spell. Here are a few of the usual unusual things that we put in there:

- Something metal. At the shop, we use iron filings, a kind of metal sawdust that's easily magnetized. If you were to run a magnet through the sand at the beach, you would find fuzzy particles clinging to it—those are tiny bits of iron. We put a dash in the base of the glass with the idea of drawing energy to the candle the way a magnet would. When I don't have iron filings, I sometimes place a regular magnet or a lodestone (a natural magnetic pebble) near the candle. Some people use change in the bottom of their candles for the same magnetic purpose, or as an offering to a particular deity in the appropriate number and denomination that the deity prefers (for example, copper pennies for Oshun, Venus, or Mercury). I'm going to use a plain disk-shaped magnet from my refrigerator and set it near the base of our moon candle.

- A sweet offering. This offering is a gift. A gesture of good faith. An invitation to sweetness. For these purposes we often use a drop of honey or molasses. If you're honoring a particular deity with your candle, or you have something else in mind, feel free to make a sweet offering of whatever seems appropriate for your purpose. It's a common practice to taste the offering first, a gesture meant to ensure that you haven't offered anything that you wouldn't take yourself. I'll use a few drops of honey for our candle.

- Incense. At this point in the process in the shop, we choose among dozens of handmade incenses and burn a small spoonful for a moment before dumping it, still smoldering, into the still empty glass container and placing a small dish on top to trap the smoke. It's very exciting and witchy, this cylinder of smoke, but the really fun part comes when you drop the dressed candle into the smoke-filled glass, causing a delightful poof effect. You can approximate this with stick incense or other forms of incense by holding the inverted glass over the stream of smoke. Of course, you'll want to do this before you put the other offerings in! It won't be quite as poofy that way, but no less magical, I promise. The recipe I have on hand for moon incense is a blend of wormwood and camphor. You might know wormwood from its star turn as the active ingredient in the allegedly hallucinogenic spirit absinthe, and camphor as the active ingredient in mothballs. I imagine they're associated with the moon because of their dizzying, sort of medicinal aromas—it's a heady blend. But I don't have any absinthe or mothballs around the house at the moment. I do have my favorite Japanese green tea incense, though. I'm not sure if it's lunar per se, but it's cool and lovely, peaceful and clean-smelling, so I'm going for it.

STEP 6: THE SPIEL

Your candle is ready! It's time for the spiel. No one makes it out of Enchantments without hearing or overhearing some version of the spiel, so I'll relay my version of it to you now.

First, we recommend that you take a salt bath before you start charging (putting your energy into) your candle. Use sea salt, Epsom salt, kosher salt, or whatever kind of salt you have. If you don't have a bathtub, dissolve some salt in a cup or bowl of water and splash it on. Go jump in the sea if you want to. The idea behind the ritual salt bath is to cleanse yourself energetically—kinda like when you wash your hands before you prepare food—to make sure you're not bringing any extraneous energy from the last thing you were doing to your new magical task.

The next thing to do is to charge your candle. When we say that, we mean finding a way to get the energy inside you into this symbolic object. The idea is to put your special mojo into the candle (which, let's all remind ourselves, is just wax with a wick), thus connecting it to your intention. Some write their intention down in detail with the candle nearby, some people dance around naked with their candle, some people meditate silently, some probably chant ancient fucking madrigals. Whatever floats your boat. One of my favorite magical practices is scanning song lyrics for lines worthy of being used as incantations in spells. When I find the right song for my intention, I freak around the house while it plays on repeat until I feel like the whole universe, and all of my neighbors, get the point already. But you do it your way. And if you have any trouble, you can listen to the Frank Sinatra song "My Way" to inspire you. Ugh. That's a terrible song example, but I think you get me.

STEP 7: LIGHT IT UP

Once the charging is done—and you'll know when it's done—light that candle up. If it goes out on its own, or if your little cousin puts it out because "it's the devil," that's fine. Just remind the candle of its task and light it up again. Let the candle burn down all the way regardless of how long it takes. Maybe you light it once a week, once a month—it doesn't matter. It stinks to leave a spell half done, though. I'm not saying you'll fall into a hell dimension if you don't finish it, just that it goes against the whole point of the thing. As above, so below! If you don't follow your real-life tasks through to completion, how can you expect your spells to work completely?

The most important thing to remember is that you can't really mess it up. It's about you and your intention. If you use the "wrong" color candle during the "wrong" phase of the moon, nothing bad will happen to you. Bad things happen because you're a mortal human on Earth, like the rest of us, and such is the shit of life. Good things happen the same way. But sometimes we can help them along with our deeds and intentions. Such is the magic.

CHAPTER 3½: SIGIL TUTORIAL

So, how do you reduce your intention down to a symbol? Good question, one that Grant Morrison answers so beautifully in an essay called "Pop Magic!" I'm hesitant to make this attempt to condense and paraphrase it, but Morrison himself was elucidating the methods of some other magical dude, Austin Osman Spare, so I guess I'll accept my role as another part of the witch's telephone chain.

A sigil is a magical symbol, a representation of the magician's intention. Any character or glyph that can evoke a complete concept can be used as, or incorporated into, a sigil: Runes from the Nordic traditions, Asian logograms (hanzi, kanji, and hanja), the letters used to write in Sanskrit or Hebrew. Other meaningful shapes and configurations of line, like stick figures, hearts, stars, horseshoes, and all the other Lucky Charms shapes, are often incorporated into sigils or just used on their own. For example, someone in need of grounding might carve the Sanskrit term for the root chakra into a dark red candle and be done with it. Or maybe they'd carve a design that resembled tree roots onto a brown candle. But for the bespoke intention of the picky witch, sometimes it pays to sigilize it yourself.

The process makes use of one of the oldest and

most alchemically transformative trios of magical tools: the pen, the paper, and the word. In fact, I suggest you sit down right now and write yourself a letter about whatever situation made you think you wanted a candle in the first place. Try to really drill down on what it is you want. Add all the specific details you can think of. Spelling doesn't count, but you're really going to want to be specific, as you'll find that magical energy tends to slip through any little loophole you leave open. Then begin to distill your intention down to a sort of elevator pitch to the universe for the desired outcome of your situation, usually a sentence beginning with "I want" or "I desire." That's your petition or declaration. Time for an example: When my partner and I had our baby, we realized that it might be helpful to have a car, the better to schlep him and all his accoutrements around town. (We live in a neighborhood where you can actually find parking for your car. I won't tell you which neighborhood that is, so that you don't come here with your car and ruin it for me.) But we were super-broke, and my man didn't think we could even afford a free car, should one magically appear. I went ahead and made this sigil anyway. People have been using sigils to envision what we want since we first started using tools. Only while we were doing it to find a wild minivan, our ancestors were calling out to mammoths. Same shit, different cave wall.

I WANT A FREE CAR

Phew, hard part is done. I figured out what I want. Now all I gotta do is scratch out all the vowels, leaving me with a string of consonants from which I will scratch out all repeated consonants until I'm left with this (although you, of course, will be left with a different string of letters):

WNTFRC

From here, I'm going to take these letters and hit 'em once more with the awesome power of my pen by arranging and combining them. Overlap and mirror. Intertwine the letters with each other, all swirly, until they look like a fancy monogram, if that's your style, or make them pointy and jagged like a metal band's logo. Just have fun doodling abstractly until you get something that looks kinda magic. You'll know when you're done tinkering. Then you can stop. Behold the sigil!

WNTFRC

Seriously, that's the only requirement: looking all rad and magic and containing your intention in a unique shape. I know, I know. I would think it was dumb, too, if I hadn't done this exact spell and then ended up being offered a big, beautiful minivan, currently enjoying its golden years, that was in fact free. Although, you know, even free costs something.

You have a sigil you're happy with. Now comes the fun part: charging it. You'll hear me refer to the process of charging something all throughout this book. It's the act of putting your intention into an image or object so that the object can help you get your vision out of your head and into your car . . . wait, that's Billy Ocean, and that song is terrifying. I meant to say that charging a magical item is the process of getting your vision out of your head and into your life. We've talked about a few ways to do this. Ecstatic dancing, or "freaking around" as I so aptly put it, is one of my favorite methods of raising energy to put into my spells, but any act that takes you out of yourself and diverts you momentarily from your mundane stream of consciousness can be used as a charging ritual for a magical item, be it herb, crystal, candle, oil, or something else altogether. In this instance we're talking about charging sigils in the Pop Magic! style, which is only one way to approach the ritual of charging, but it's so much fun I wouldn't want you to miss it. I'm going to turn you over to my man Grant Morrison for this because (a) he's the shit, (b) I'm very shy—you should know this about me by now—and (c) I'd be hard-pressed to do a better job of describing what he so lovingly called the "wank technique."

Some non-magicians, I've noticed, convulse with nervous laughter whenever I mention the word "masturbation." . . . Be that as it may, magical masturbation is actually more fun and, equally, more serious, than the secular hand shandy, and all it requires is this: at the moment of orgasm, you must see the image of your chosen sigil blazing before the eyes in your mind and project it outwards into the ethereal mediaspheres and logoverses where desires swarm and condense into flesh. The sigil can be written on paper, on your hand or your chest, on the forehead of a lover or wherever you think it will be most effective.

At the white-hot instant of orgasm, consciousness blinks. Into this blink, this abyssal crack in perception, a sigil can be launched . . . However . . . one does not change the universe simply by masturbating . . . If that were true, every vague fantasy we had in our heads at the moment of orgasm would come true within months. Intent is what makes the difference here.

—From Grant Morrison, "Pop Magic!," in *Book of Lies: The Disinformation Guide to Magick and the Occult*, ed. Richard Metzger (Disinformation Books, 2014)

So! Go on and do that . . . I'll wait.

Once the sigil is charged up, however you've chosen to do the charging, the next step is to release it, which basically means destroy or dispose of it. This is yet another opportunity to get creative with your newfound witchy knowledge and devise an original and ritually appropriate way to ditch your sigil. There's that flaming cauldron method I mentioned earlier, but that is, admittedly, kind of a lot. When I'm looking for metaphorically appropriate ideas, I usually start with the elements and what I know about their connotations. Earth: work, material things. Air: matters of thought. Water: the feeeeelings. Fire: the actions, the will.

So, you made a love sigil already, even though I was about to tell you not to, right? (See Chapter 9.) Of course you did. Do as thou wilt, but this shit actually works, so keep that in mind. Maybe you can dispose of it in running water, as is recommended with a lot of wishing-type spells. (Show a body of water to a human person and they'll make a wish and throw something in it: a wishing well, a wishing bridge, the fountain at the mall.) The idea there is to borrow a little bit of energy for your spell by allowing the motion of the currents to carry your intention off into the unknown. And yes, the toilet counts as running water. And yes, I have flushed sigils down the toilet before. But to be fair, the spells had to do with my house and home, so I figured sending my wishes through the plumbing, the very bowels of the place, seemed appropriate.

Money spell? That's material! Maybe you wanna bury it. Maybe you wanna bury it in the open construction pit outside your job or bank branch. Looking for artistic inspiration? Maybe that sigil gets released at the top of the Ferris wheel to float away into the ether, where ideas form like weather. Maybe you're trying to be done with something or someone forever, so you decide to burn your sigil while crying your eye makeup off and listening to the song that makes you cry your eye makeup off—for the last time! Go full melodrama if you want, or keep it real simple. If you choose to carve your sigil on a candle, that spell will be released with fire. Fire is about action, so it serves as an excellent reminder to be sure that your actions match your intentions.

These are all just options, but get rid of it already! And do your best to forget about it for a while. Relax and let it happen. *A watched cauldron never bubbles*, they always say. Just kidding. Nobody ever says that.

SUGGESTED READING

Richard Metzger, ed., *Book of Lies: The Disinformation Guide to Magick and the Occult* (Disinformation Books, 2014)

Grant Morrison, *Supergods* (Spiegel & Grau, 2011)

Lady Rhea, *The Enchanted Candle* (self-published, 1986)

Michael G. Lloyd, *Bull of Heaven* (Asphodel Press, 2012)

Chapter 4

THE HERB TALK, OR PLANTS AND MINERALS

There comes a time in every young witch's life when they're faced with the decision of whether or not to experiment with herbs. Don't feel like you need to give in to peer pressure from your little herb-head friends. You don't have to do herbs just to be cool, although herbal magic and herbal medicine are, in fact, *quite* cool. In the millennia of human life that existed before or outside the reach of what we know now as Western medicine, medicine and magic were often intimately interwoven concepts. But before we get any further, I'd like to make one essential distinction between herbal medicine and herbal magic: only some people, highly trained and licensed herbalists, are qualified to recommend that you ingest some of the more powerful herbs, and in what quantity and with what caveats. I'm not one of those highly trained people, so most of the herbs and plants I'll describe in this chapter will fall safely and obviously within the category of foodstuffs. And even then, most of these applications are meant for the outside of your body. When in doubt, the outside is the safer side.

A plant's magical property, or its *vibration*, is its particular expression of the energy that animates all living things. For example, an orange's sweet taste, eye-catching color, and juiciness express its aliveness differently than, say, a sprig of mint's green, leafy, tingly aspects; oranges and mint *vibrate* at different frequencies. Categorizing herbs by their distinct vibrations and then using them ritually to support an intention is what herbal magic is all about. In fact, combining herbs in their different forms (leaf, bark, root, flower, fruit, or essential oil) is the basis of a lot of the "craft" part of witchcraft. The oils, incenses, baths, et cetera, that we make at the shop and that you can find in a million spell books are all built on herb lore, that is, the stories of how people use, or once used, herbs for magic. It's a craft learned over time and with much study, ideally through an apprenticeship to a master of some kind. But don't fret—there's plenty you can do with a witches' herbal and a little ingenuity.

Herb lore can be complicated, and even if you're lucky enough to have access to an apothecary or essential oil shop, it can also be prohibitively expensive to amass the ingredients for some spells you might find in a book or online. But spells don't have to be complicated to be effective. All you need are the proper reference materials to figure out which plants might lend themselves to your purpose. A good herbal can be especially useful if you're trying to follow a complex spell recipe and you need to substitute with something that has a similar vibe. If you're anything like me, though, you might also find yourself using it to look up the uses of the herbs, oils and flowers you might already have around the house, as inspiration to make the spell you need with the stuff you have.

What I'm gonna do for you, 'cause I'm nice, is list a few relatively-easy-to-gather herbs and spices along with their magical uses, and in some cases fun facts! If you don't have a magic garden, an apothecary, botánica, or occult shop, maybe there's a health food store, some place with a large array of teas and essential oils, or even a nursery or florist in your town. These places will be especially good resources for your magical materials, but most of the stuff I'll list should be available at your basic grocery store. Remember, the most useful magical tools are the ones you can get your hands on, so you don't have to get hung up on your spikenards and mandrakes and what-have-you if they're out of reach.

I just performed a little shakedown of my spice rack, medicine cabinet, and window box for magical supplies, and I found a handful of common kitchen-witching items so we can discuss their potential ritual purposes.

CRUSHED RED PEPPER

PLANET: MARS
ELEMENT: FIRE

Most peppers and spicy things are associated with Mars because of its active, fiery vibe.
It's sometimes sprinkled around the perimeter of a space for uncrossing or banishing negativity by metaphorically burning it off. (Black pepper can be used similarly to ward off bad vibes and ill-intentioned people.) Sprinkling it protectively

around the perimeter of the home is one way to employ this element's power.

ROSES

PLANET: VENUS
ELEMENT: WATER

Roses are used for love and luck. With food-grade rosebuds, you can make rosebud tea to induce prophetic dreams of your love future. Rose oil and perfume are used to attract love, and rosewater is considered an appropriate ritual cleansing agent to use before doing your love magic. The powerfully attractive scent and energy of rose petals also make them useful in luck drawing mixtures.

SOMETHING COMPLETELY DIFFERENT

By contrast, Asafetida is the most horrible-smelling item in the whole apothecary. Derived from a giant varietal of fennel, it usually comes in the form of a powder. We call it "ass-o-fetid-a" because it smells like fetid ass rolled in the everything from an everything bagel and singed hair. Because of its raw horror aroma, it's used for banishing and exorcism. That's right—it smells so terrible that even *evil* gets offended. And yet, despite the raw horror aroma, it's delicious! Often referred to as Hing, it's a staple of Indian vegetarian cooking. When heated, the asafetida mellows into something oniony and nourishing.

CHAMOMILE

PLANET: SUN
ELEMENT: WATER

You know that stuff's crazy calming and soothing in a tea or incense, but between you and me, it's
nice in a smoking blend mixed with other smokable herbs,
and it's just as pleasant sprinkled in the bath (or maybe keep
it in the tea bag to avoid the mess). The gentle scent will chill
you out. Chamomile is another herb that you can sprinkle
around the perimeter of your home for protection and purification. It seems to have the same mellowing effect no matter
how you use it.

ROSEMARY

PLANET: SUN
ELEMENT: FIRE

Rosemary has a stimulating, activating scent. It's used for
a whole litany of things, magically speaking, but protection
during travel stands out as a particularly apt application.
Wearing a chaplet (similar to a flower crown) of rosemary is
supposed to improve your memory, and drinking rosemary
tea is said to help with mental acuity, so this one is starting
to sound like a perfect study aid.

LEMON

PLANET: MOON
ELEMENT: WATER

Lemon is not technically an herb, but its juice and oil are powerful energetic cleansers. You can use lemon to clean the vibes of stones and crystals, or any item for magical use. Lemon is also a powerful astringent; astringents cause your pores to constrict, so they're useful for cleansing the skin. I use a cut lemon covered in salt in the bath or shower for a simple energetic cleansing scrub.

SAGE

PLANET: VENUS
ELEMENT: EARTH

The sage I'm referring to here is sagebrush, or white sage, not the sage you'd have in your average herb garden. Maybe you don't have any just lying around, but I always do, usually in the form of a smudge stick, or a little bundle of it in the shape of a cigar, tied with string. It's a native American plant, burned for its purifying smoke in a smudging ceremony, a very particular ritual that is employed for spiritual cleansing purposes. This is not the same as just filling your home with sage smoke, although the intentions are similar.

CINNAMON

PLANET: SUN
ELEMENT: FIRE

The scent of cinnamon is attractive and bright (solar), and also spicy and stimulating (fire). Cinnamon oil was held sacred by most of the ancient civilizations we've been discussing here: Greeks, Egyptians, Romans, and ancient Jews. When used as an anointing oil or incense, it's meant to increase the frequency of spiritual vibes. Its sweet, spicy aroma is often used in love magic, or as an offering to any of the numerous love goddesses who agree that it's delicious, including Oshun, Aphrodite, and Brigid.

CLOVE

PLANET: JUPITER
ELEMENT: FIRE

You can burn powdered clove to stop people from talking shit about you. See, I promised you fun facts, and now I've delivered! Although the factual nature of this claim is dubious, clove oil does in fact have a numbing effect when you put it in your mouth, so maybe that's the source of the association. Can't talk shit with a numb tongue. If you try it out, let me know. As a Jupiterian spice, it can also be used in spells of growth and expansion including but not limited to your financial situation.

LAVENDER

PLANET: MERCURY
ELEMENT: AIR

Oh, lavender. Is it fair to hate you because others love you too well? I feel like it's in so many things: tea, dish soap, cookies, sweater drawers, and bubble bath. What's it *not* used for? It's similarly versatile magically speaking, as it's included in mixtures for attracting love and was worn as perfume by Renaissance-era sex workers to advertise their services, but ironically, during the same period it was also thought to preserve a maid's chastity (along with rosemary). An association of more recent vintage is the one you already know: promoting peace and relaxation.

LET'S PLAY "NETTE OR NETTLE?"

NETTLE (STINGING)

PLANET: MARS
ELEMENT: FIRE

Nettle is a purificatory herb carried in the hand or burned to drive away negative influences. Nette is my friend and manager at Enchantments. Outside of the apothecary, nettle is most commonly found in the kind of tea bag that says something inspirational on the tag. Outside of the apothecary, Nette is most likely to be found playing Scrabble or dancing lasciviously. Both Nette and nettle are associated with the energy of the planet Mars—they're active (stinging counts as pretty active for a plant) and they're both excellent purifying agents in a fiery, abrasive sort of way. Nettle's powerful, spiky vibes can be used to promote fiery lust. Banishing evil and promoting fiery lust also happen to be the preferred pastimes of dear Nette, of whom you have heard and will hear quite a bit in these pages.

Two less common items that are worth mentioning are the most popular resins, frankincense and myrrh, which might be familiar to you from a certain infant's baby shower. You may remember from Chapter 1 that resins are hardened drops of tree sap that are very aromatic when burned.

FRANKINCENSE

PLANET: SUN
ELEMENT: FIRE

When you look up the spiritual uses of frankincense, the books basically just say "spiritual uses"—that is, all of them. Its smoke is used to purify and sanctify a space and to uplift the spiritual energy for meditation and worship. It's the basis of many magical formulas in honor of the sun and solar deities. The ancient Egyptians burned frankincense at dawn to honor the return of the sun god, Ra.

MYRRH

PLANET: MOON
ELEMENT: WATER

The perfect elemental balance to frankincense, myrrh is similarly used for ritual purification and spiritual elevation. More often than not you'll find the two blended together.

SALT

PLANET: EARTH
ELEMENT: EARTH

My favorite mineral. Hands down. I'm crazy for the stuff. It's one of the most commonly used magical ingredients, owing to its cleansing and grounding powers. This is quite a natural association to make, as salt is of the earth. The ocean and our bodily fluids—sweat, tears, blood, urine, even the amniotic fluid that sustains life in the womb—are to one degree or another composed of salt. Your local pickle purveyor can tell you that the salt in the brine preserves the pickle and inhibits the growth of harmful bacteria. Many of us use a saline solution to gently cleanse and irrigate our eyes, mouths, and nasal passages. These quotidian but no less miraculous uses lend themselves to salt's common magical usage as a purifying agent. As you know by now, salt is often used to symbolize the element earth on an altar, and can be sprinkled around the perimeter of your home or any other space that you wish to consecrate. At the shop we suggest cleansing yourself with salt, usually in a bath, as a way to prepare for doing a ritual, but you can give the same salt bath to your crystals or other magical implements.

SPEAKING OF WHICH, WHAT SHOULD I DO WITH THIS ROCK?

- Clean it. Most people will tell you that it's important to ritually cleanse any stone that you plan to use for magic before you use it, the supposition being that your crystal had a long and mysterious journey in getting to you, and everyone likes to wash up after a long journey. Whether or not you have magical intentions for them, crystals and gems are captivating. I mean, we're talking about straight-up treasures, and the Earth doesn't give up her gem treasures all that easily. Unless you found it yourself, you don't know where your stone came from and what happened along the way. So you cleanse it. Some people like to set it out in the sunlight and count on the purifying power of the sun to clear any negativity. Some people use moonlight. Some give them a little salt water bath, and others devise their own rituals to cleanse their stones with the power of one element or another: burying in earth, leaving them in a small net in a stream of moving water, or running them briefly through purifying smoke, like sage, or through the flame of a candle.

- Charge it. Once your crystal is all squeaky clean you may want to charge it with your intention the same way you would charge a candle, a sigil, an herb, or a talisman. As you'll discover when you do your own stone research, each type of crystal is associated with multiple uses. It's up to you to find a way to let the crystal know what you want it to do. This is a subtle thing—it may not look like much more than holding it in your hand while you visualize yourself achieving the state you mean to promote with the use of the crystal. Prosperous. Loved and loving. Healthy. Peaceful and safe from harm.

- Use it. When your stone is charged with its purpose, you can use it in any way that's concordant with your goals. If you're doing love-drawing magic, you might put it in your pocket when you go to an event or a party where you're likely to run into eligible folks. If you're burning a money-drawing candle, you might bring some gold and green stones to add to your altar array. My friend Caroline, who did the kick-ass illustrations in this book, tells me she likes to meditate with them placed at different energy points on her body. Some witches add crystals to their baths (as long as they're not toxic—you gotta check). And some go all the way there and use crystal sex toys and something called a yoni egg that . . . I just can't. I'm sure it's cool. Maybe you should try it. But I can't.

MIX 'EM UP

A readily doable form of herb magic you might try your hand at is the making of an ouanga bag. At least that's what we call them at Enchantments, after the term used in Voodoo. In Hoodoo, it's referred to as a mojo, mojo bag, mojo hand, conjure bag, root bag, gris-gris, charm bag, or any of the endless variations thereupon. Whatever you want to call it, it's an excellent way for the novice and expert alike to combine herbs, stones, resins, pieces of scripture, and other talismanic or magically resonant items into a conveniently portable spell. It's such a popular type of magic because it's an intimate and discreet method of carrying magic you might want to keep secret and have with you at all times.

In Hoodoo traditions, the bag itself is usually made of red flannel, but feel free to use cloth of the color and texture that suit your purpose. Maybe your love ouanga is red silk, while your money ouanga is made of green hemp. Once you've collected the herbs and other magical things that align with your intention, the next step is to ritualistically bind them to the intention you've set. Like all rituals you devise yourself, this can be as complicated and theatrical, or as simple and utilitarian, as you want it to be: just do what it takes to get your mojo into that mojo bag. Many traditions maintain that once the ouanga bag is charged or consecrated, it should be worn close to the skin and concealed from the passing gaze of others. Although not all spell bags bear the same restrictions, it's generally thought of as a thing to be kept private. Carry it with you and let it work its magic, bolstering your intention as you go through the day.

SUGGESTED READING

Scott Cunningham, *Cunningham's Encyclopedia of Magical Herbs* (Llewellyn, 1984)

Scott Cunningham, *Magical Herbalism* (Llewellyn, 1986)

Scott Cunningham, *Cunningham's Encyclopedia of Crystal, Gem and Metal Magic* (Llewellyn, 1988)

Chapter 5

WANDERING STARS, OR PLANETS

A whole bunch of humans, for countless generations, have collectively chosen to characterize the solar system as a pantheon of planetary archetypes that exemplify the range of human expression. In this chapter, you'll find a breakdown of the associations upon which we base a lot of the witchy decisions we make when we're putting together a spell. Each of the nine planets (witches still fux with Pluto), plus the moon and the sun, has a certain personality. Once you get your head around them, you'll have a better idea of why a witch might use a Mars candle for sexual attraction or weight loss but not necessarily for healing or drawing money, or why some spells might be recommended for a particular phase of the moon, or what the hell everyone's moaning about when they talk about Mercury going retrograde.

THE LUMINARIES

The moon and the sun are counted among the planets when we're talking about astrology, but as part of a subcategory called luminaries, or light bodies. The sun signifies the self, the ego, the center of your existence. As metaphors go, it's almost disappointingly literal. *The sun is the center of our existence? You don't say!* Solar energy is used for cleansing, inspiring joy, and attracting attention. The moon, on the other hand, is the more reflective (again, literally, since it reflects the light of the sun), introspective sort of energy. It's about how one relates to one's emotions and interiority. The moon is often used to concentrate energy around the home, the internal self, and the deeper depths of feeling. We'll get into this more when we look at our birth charts (see Chapter 12).

THE INNER PLANETS

Mercury

Mercury is mercurial (duh), quick of wit, and tricky, too. The first in line among the planets, Mercury is the one who makes the introductions and the connections. Mercury wins the race around the sun every single time, at a record speed of eighty-eight days per orbit, which, I assume, is the reason the god Mercury, aka Hermes, is depicted with wings on his cap and sandals. We're asking for Mercury's favor every single waking second of the day, since he presides over commerce, communication, and technology, and most of us are attached to our phones and computers, obsessed with sharing every thought that drifts through the transom of our minds with the whole world at the same time, constantly hitting that Mercury button to get another dose of connectivity. Hence the freaking out when Mercury is retrograde (i.e., appears from our vantage point to be moving backward as compared with its usual path across the sky), temporarily interrupting its regularly scheduled programming and crashing your laptop. Honestly, it's a complete wonder that Mercury doesn't flip us off more often. Dude needs a break sometimes; we all do. I say: Do you, Mercury! Treat yo'self. Take a little retrograde vacation, and leave us all to just deal with waiting the full sixty seconds for some bullshit video to load.

Since it's the planet of communication and commerce, when it's moving backward, some folks think it's not the time to start new stuff, sign contracts, or make any big transactions. But I'll tell you that I signed my contract for this book when Mercury was retrograde, and everything was fine. There's no need to freak out; just do your best to work *with* and not against it. It's good to be aware of the associations, and reflective about what they might mean to us, without descending into superstition and paranoia. With that in mind, when Mercury is retrograde it's a good time to finish up stuff that you've already started, review your progress, and integrate your lessons where communication is concerned.

Venus

Then there's Venus. You know her: she's the femme next door. She's so hot, but flirtatiously out of reach. In astrological systems, the planet Venus is the pinnacle of beauty and love. Compared to Mercury, it has a languid orbital pace: it takes 224.7 days to complete its route around the sun. It also takes its sweet ass time to rotate on its own axis: there are only two days per year on Venus. It's the only planet in the solar system that spins clockwise; all the others rotate counterclockwise (as seen from Earth). Isn't that fascinating? Why didn't I learn that in school? Shit, I'm sorry, Mr. Zeller. I bet you tried to teach me that in high school astronomy class, but it went in one ear and out the other. (Class took place in an actual planetarium, so spacing out was a common occurrence.) Venus appears in the sky here and there, like an artfully placed beauty mark, at morning twilight *and* evening twilight, all wabi-sabi and adorable. So hot! But, like, approachable. This is the energy we tap into for . . . you guessed it: love magic! You get no points for guessing, because that should be obvious by now.

Mars

Okay, no more messing around. Planet Mars refuses to beat around the bush. Mars would rather beat you up than beat around the bush. Mars puts its head down and charges horns-first at . . . well, I don't know . . . anything. Whatchu got? In the bullring, Mars is the red cape and the ring and the bull *and* all the people in the stands getting hot for the *sheer unholy* joy of conflict. Martian energy is that redness we discussed earlier, that testosterone-filled get-up-and-go. It's hot for work, for sex, for passionate movement and exertion, for gesticulation of all kinds. Please see the entry in Chapter 2 on the color red, where I got a little carried away with the concept, and insert all that fiery shit here. Mars the planet is, in fact, red, as we now know for sure from data collected by NASA, the result of a high concentration of oxidized iron or rust in the surface dust. Not that the ancient Egyptian priest/ess astronomers knew that when they dubbed it the "Red One." They were going by its relatively red hue when compared to the other stars and planets in the sky.

Earth

Earth should be an easy one to remember, but personally, I end up neglecting its energies pretty often, by forgetting to eat (so stupid, I don't even understand), not getting enough rest, or otherwise failing to attend to the physicality of things. You might not have noticed this about me, but I'm somewhat preoccupied with the ethereal! Earth magic is about grounding— the magic of feeling steady and whole and rooted in your time and place, maintaining links to the past and reaching tendrils into the future. Earth magic is about turning off the part of your mind that insists erroneously that you're some kind of autonomous being that stands distinct from other beings. One of the most grounding ritual activities that I do is practicing yoga, where we usually chant *om*, the mantra or sound of all living things! At once! The hum total of all of creation. Thanks again to NASA, we can see the oneness of Earth very clearly. I mean, what is a living planet like this one but a single organism floating inside an invisible bubble of protection from the vastness of space? As far as we know, this is the only planet with anything growing, so we tap into the strength of that connection when we're navigating tough emotional terrain, when we need stability, or when we're looking for signs of abundance and fertility made possible by our unique position in time and space.

Jupiter

♃

Jupiter is the big one, and don't you forget it. It has more than twice the mass of all the other planets combined, and it's got gravitas! It's the boss planet. The astrological concept here is growth, expansion, authority, and rulership. It's associated with Zeus and Thor and all those big butch-type daddy gods. It's mostly gas. I imagine a room filled with cigar smoke, the sounds of gregarious conversation, back-slapping, and mutually beneficial deals. Its planetary energy is also associated with higher education in the institutional sense, fraternities (that's a Greek system, after all), and foreign travel for educational purposes. It's all very collegiate, referring to the systems of merit and hierarchy, but also the partying part of the stereotypical undergrad experience: Jupiter can be the planet of merriment to excess. Asking for Jupiter's favors is like asking for positive attention or approval from an authority in your field. The nod from up top. Cross-reference with the color purple.

THE DEVIL

There's no devil, per se, in a lot of polytheistic systems. There isn't much of a need for one. Each archetype comes complete with its own shadow side. Zeus is power and authority, and that's great, right? But guess what: he's a rapist (of Leda, Callisto, and Alcmene, to name a few). Aphrodite is the epitome of beauty and love and sexy times, and everyone knows it, but that doesn't stop her from transforming innocent people into all manner of beasts and starting epic wars (like the Trojan one) to serve her vain jealousy. Who needs a devil when the gods fuck up so much just by being their own divine selves?

Saturn

Saturn, on the other hand, is about limitation and restriction. Up until 1781, Saturn was the most distant observable planet, the edge of the known solar system, so it came to represent, well, *death! the end! the edge of the abyss!* or, less hysterically, boundaries and control, often punctuated by the hard stop of mortality. You can think of any of these planetary archetypes as teachers (please do—that's kinda the whole point of this), but Saturn is the teacher in the kung fu movies who makes you do menial tasks endlessly with no praise and no assurance of advancement, but then after a long montage has passed, you, the chosen one, find that what you thought was a slog through the shit was actually the essential, specific, and perfect training for the challenges that lie ahead. Saturn is the "thank me later" planet. Saturn dispels illusions, cuts through the bullshit. Nette shared an incredibly wise thing the other day to this effect: she praised a regular customer by saying, "See, you're smart enough to know that just because things aren't going *your* way, it doesn't mean they're going the *wrong* way." That's Saturn's gift: the lesson you didn't want and didn't know you needed.

Saturn carves a huge orbital swath through the sky, so it takes about twenty-nine years to return to the position it was in when you were born. This phenomenon is referred to astrologically as your first Saturn return, and it's considered a sort of Rubicon in terms of maturity. It's the time when you're faced with the full hit of adulthood, when a lot of bodies begin to show the first signs of revolt against whatever abuse you may have heaped upon them in your youth. Saturn is the lesson implicit in the hangover. You don't *have* to take the lesson, but if you don't, you'll repeat it. So we use Saturnine vibes for the purposes of drawing or highlighting the firm boundaries in our lives, and for banishing negative or useless energy. Imagine Cher from *Moonstruck* slapping you across the face and saying, "Snap out of it!" and you'll get the idea.

THE OUTER PLANETS

Uranus

Uranus is the first of the outer, or modern, planets. Old-school traditions don't deal a whole lot with these planets, because they didn't have much, if anything, to go on: these three planets are super far away and weren't discovered until much later. Because of this, some folks like to talk about outer planetary associations in terms of refinements or tweaks on the vibes of inner planets. Where Venus is about attraction and communion, Uranus is about standing out and being apart. Where Mars is about winning the game, Uranus is about changing the game. Uranus is a revolutionary planet. Its purview is the overthrowing of established orders, visionary fervor, and breaking with tradition and convention, sometimes in flagrant ways. As if to make that point abundantly clear, Uranus is also hung funny in the sky; it's oriented almost perpendicular to the other planets. If Uranus had a flag, it would be a freak flag. I mean, they almost named it Herschel, for Christ's sake, or more precisely, for the sake of its discovering astronomer, William Herschel. Mercury, Venus, Earth, Mars, Jupiter, Saturn, and *Herschel?* Seriously? Those for whom Uranus features prominently in their natal chart are said to have the traits of an iconoclast. Shifts in Uranus's position relative to Earth mark epochs and generations, because it takes about eighty-four years for it to complete its route around the sun; as a result, it has a similar position in the charts of people who are born within a few years of each other.

Neptune

Neptune is the Vaseline on the lens of the solar system. It's got that nice, gauzy soft focus, like when your pupils are dilated. Neptune is negatively associated with illusion and escapism (this means drugs), but positively it is the patron planet of all you dreamers out there dreaming your dreams of a better world. As you can tell from the god Neptune's trident, it has a pretty watery vibe. Neptune was only discovered in the 1800s, so it doesn't have much in the way of ancient associations, but fantasy, imagination, and visionary creativity are what it has come to represent. Neptune is the domain of dreams, both the revealing kind and the illusory variety. Neptune is the emblem of the subconscious mind, or the subconscious of a group or a culture as expressed through its underlying mythos—the stories that we tell ourselves, and the stories we tell about ourselves. It travels slowly around the sun, like Uranus, so it stays in the same sign for long enough to have a similar effect on a generation of people, influencing the resonant themes of that generation's cultural output. Neptune teaches you how to accept a seemingly impossible thing as possible. It's a beautiful vision, but as with any fantasy, it's up to you whether you use it to inspire or delude yourself.

Pluto

♇

And, Pluto! The end! I know we said Saturn was the end, but we were just kidding. Pluto's really the end. Named for the god of the underworld, Pluto is the reaper. But don't fear it.

Pluto remains mysterious in part due to the fact that it was only discovered in 1930, and because it has a tremendously long and kinda busted orbit that doesn't behave anything like that of the other planets (which is one of the reasons it's no longer considered a planet). Its orbit around the sun has been calculated to take about 250 years, but since they only discovered it 90 years ago, I'll believe that when I see it. In astrology, Pluto is supposed to mark the beginnings and endings of different periods of your life; where it appears in your chart signifies the area of life in which you'll have major, 180-degree changes in how you approach things. But by the time we get to Pluto, way out here at the end of the solar system, my understanding gets a little spotty. People at the shop would have stopped me hours ago if I went on this long about the planets.

All of these associations will help us in Chapter 12 as we try to understand the signs of the zodiac, each of which derives its characteristics from one or more of these planetary influences. And if none of this is clicking for you, don't worry. These systems are meant to help you add layers of resonance to your spell work, not fill you with interplanetary anxiety.

Chapter 6

WHEEL OF THE YEAR, OR THE CALENDAR

As in any religion, the modern Pagan festival calendar is a way of organizing the community around a celebration of shared values. The turning of the seasons is the through line of collective Wiccan practice, but tons of people who wouldn't necessarily identify as Wiccans or witches find value in this alternative festival calendar as a way of honoring the change of seasons without defaulting to one's family of origin or the dominant culture's religious expression. The way I was raised, our springtime celebrations were secular Easter (eggs, candy, family dinner, no church) and Passover (parsley, horseradish, bread of affliction, no temple). Both were enjoyable in their own way, but neither truly inspired in me the wonder of the season, so I had to invent my own holiday for that purpose. I call it Día de los Dresses. The date wanders from year to year depending on the fluctuations of the climate, but it's the first day that it's warm enough to wear a dress with bare legs and all the femmes in the city float around like sugarplum fairies and take selfies with the cherry blossoms. I'm one of those ladies! Best day of the year. It tends to fall somewhere between the Pagan celebrations of Ostara (vernal equinox) and Beltane (May Day), as we'll go on to talk more about, but the point is that the wheel of the year provides a framework for celebrating change, and indicates some ideas for rituals to focus on the themes inspired by the natural world. But when in doubt, it's safe to say that any of the festivals we'll explore in this chapter could be correctly observed with a bonfire and feast, since that's what the word "festival" means. I'll talk more about the particulars of the Pagan calendar in a sec, but first let's look into the magical vestiges that remain in the belligerently mundane Gregorian calendar that we all use today.

DAYS OF THE WEEK

In Romance languages, the planet/deity association underlying each day is more etymologically obvious (the Italian word for Wednesday, *mercoledì*, sounds like "Mercury" for a reason), but since English is a composite language, we sometimes have to do a little digging to get to them. Sunday is the sun's day, Monday is moon day, and Saturday is for Saturn. Clear enough. Tuesday, Wednesday, Thursday, and Friday are derived from the names of Norse deities: Tyr, a war god similar to Mars, lends his name to Tuesday; Wodin's (aka Odin's) dominion over communication, art, and poetry has him synchronized with Mercury and Wednesday; Thursday is Thor's day; and either Frigg and/or Freya (folks don't agree), goddesses often thought of in the same love realm as Venus, lend their names to Friday.

SABBATS

Of course, the witchy underpinnings of the common calendar go much deeper. Many Wiccan and Pagan groups mark the beginning or midpoint of the four seasons that we all already know. The eight festival seasons, or *sabbats*, that constitute the sacred wheel of the year are a mash-up of a variety of European folk holidays and observances that date back to before dates. They didn't begin existence as a coherent, contiguous tradition; rather, as different cultures overlapped, an amalgamated celebration calendar developed for the purpose of shared festivity within a heterogeneous community. As the Roman Empire swept across continents, it adapted its own religious festivals to include the festivals of the occupied people. This is just to say that virtually all of these holidays with tricky-to-spell, arcane-sounding names will, once explained, feel pretty familiar to you. Like, creepily familiar.

Samhain

We'll begin the year with Samhain (pronounced "sow-when"). Happy witchy new year! Samhain takes place on the last day of October, aka Halloween, aka All Hallows' Eve, the night before All Saints' Day. It's a cross-quarter day, which is another way of saying a day that marks the midpoint of a season rather than its beginning or end. October 31 (or thereabouts) is situated right in the middle of autumn, between the autumnal equinox in September and the winter solstice in December. You probably know a little something about this festival, because it's the time of year you're most likely to be reminded of the existence of witches, and you're clearly at least a little bit interested in witches. Samhain season marks the death of the year: the leaves fall, and the last solid harvest is brought in—hence the pumpkins for carving, apples for bobbing, and corn (of the maze, maize, and candy varieties). Goths rejoice at the return of the long nights and trench coat weather. For us at the store, Samhain is a time of crowded aisles and random inquiries about the great beyond.

It's said that during Samhain season, the veil between life and death is at its thinnest and most permeable. This makes it a traditional time to honor our ancestors and departed loved ones. Cultures from every corner of the globe take the seasonal cue to contemplate mortality and whatever is or could be beyond the world that we see. Ancestor worship is a powerful sort of magic. It's a gratitude practice, not a transaction; it involves no wishing or willing because all of that already happened. Your ancestors willed their bloodline into the future, and they succeeded, because here *you* are, your ancestors' wildest dream. That's something to light a candle to. All across the Americas, seasonal rituals of ancestor worship take place around this same time of year, some based in indigenous traditions and some based in European (both Christian and otherwise) festivals. All serve the same purpose of honoring and caring for our dead by tending their graves or otherwise creating altars with gifts in offering to the departed. (Note: In the Southern Hemisphere, they do the same kind of things to honor their dead but in the opposite part of the calendar year, because the seasons are reversed.)

The "dressing up and going door-to-door in search of treats" element of the festival comes from mumming, an old Celtic tradition where people would go around the town in costume, reciting mischievous poems in exchange for food and drink. Something like "Trick or treat, smell my feet, give me something good to eat," but hopefully with a more ancient and portentous follow-up than "If you don't, I don't care, I'll pull down your underwear." But I'm no historian. Did they even have underwear back then, in this hazily imagined antiquity?

Another costume tradition of the season with a totally separate origin is the *calavera* (skull) makeup that people don for Día de los Muertos, which is intended not to scare your neighbors into giving you candy but rather to resonate with the *calaveras de azucar* (sugar skulls) that are used as decorative offerings to dead loved ones. They remind us of how sweet and temporary life is.

However you celebrate it, a festival season that ritualizes our connections to our dead, our gratitude for their lives and our own in all their impermanence, and a commemoration of the seasons passing from light into darkness is a good thing. So what's your Samhain-time ritual gonna look like? I suggest choosing a lost loved one, ancestor or not. Think of the sort of food or drink they liked. Or their signature scent. Or maybe you possess an item of theirs, or a photo. Make a space in your home to assemble these items and light a candle while enjoying their faves. Set some aside to leave in offering, either on your altar or someplace outside, especially if there's a place that's particularly resonant with that person's memory. If Grandpa liked old-fashioned candy like Mr. Goodbar, and menthols, and lotto, then you better get yourself over to the corner store and stock up on the magical supplies to do some ancestor worship.

And while you're out there, pick up some chrysanthemums. From what I can tell, chrysanthemums are integral to most festivals of ancestor worship. Maybe it's just another fall thing or maybe the dead have a collective favorite flower, but some variety of chrysanthemum or another from the family Asteraceae are involved in festivals of ancestor worship from enough different places that I have to note it here: marigolds for Día de los Muertos, giant potted mums that people put out beside the jack-o'-lanterns in the suburbs, or the large flowers you find in traditional Chinese paintings. In parts of China and Japan, some people celebrate Double Nine Day (ninth day of the ninth month according to the Chinese calendar, usually in October), a day that has too much *yang* (active, intense, overt energy), so precautions are to be taken in the form of climbing a tall mountain and wearing and drinking chrysanthemum to cool things down. It is also a moment to tend to the graves of loved ones and leave offerings of special foods. Sound familiar? Of course it does. Our spiritual needs are so similar that we tend to address them in a similar fashion, as we'll reiterate when we discuss . . .

Yule

Good ol' Yule. Yule is celebrated on and around the winter solstice. It's the season of the shortest days, but also the season that contains the first days to begin to lengthen again. We take this festival to celebrate light, what little of it we have in terms of sunshine, and what we can make for ourselves through shared warmth and jollity. The European Pagan and folk traditions of the season included wassailing, which is an arcane tradition of drinking sweet hot alcohol while singing and bothering your neighbors. Oh, wait, that's caroling. There were also shocking reports of people decorating evergreen trees, and chestnuts roasting on an open fire! You know what

I'm about to say, but you're not going to like it. It's just like Christmas! *Christmas!* A lot of those old-timey Christmasy things you've seen painted on a tin of cookies come from old Druid and Germanic traditions that predate Christianity. Mistletoe? It's one of the only green things to be found in the winter in the frozen north. Its stubborn refusal to die under those circumstances is a mark of a pretty powerful plant, so it was held sacred among the Druids. The oranges spiked with cloves? They're meant to remind you of the sun and its glorious gradual return from the underworld.

It's kind of weird to me that people choose to celebrate the birth of a baby outdoors in the desert in the fall or summer with a frozen Nordic winter-themed party, but it's cool. That just goes to show you the deep human need for lights and parties around this time of year. I wouldn't want to spoil things for Christians and Pagans alike by irreverently suggesting that they are doing the same damn thing around this time of year, for ever so slightly different reasons. Some of us are turning up in the snow to honor the return of our sun god, while others of us are turning up in the snow to honor the son of God. As long as we're all of us partying a path through the longest nights of the year, it's semantics to me.

What's next is . . .

Imbolc

It's another cross-quarter day, the height of a season, at that peak point of winter where you can begin to see over the hump. Spring finally seems like it could be a reality. A world without parkas could exist again. Imbolc celebrates and welcomes the thaw; it's a ritual time of looking forward. By now it shouldn't surprise you that Groundhog Day, a secularized prognostication holiday if ever there was one, occurs around Imbolc. When seeking signs of spring, it seems, we'll take 'em from whatever crocuses or giant rodents happen to cross our path.

Imbolc is also associated with rituals of welcoming and preparing, as if for an honored guest. In this case, the guest is Brigid. Brigid is the Celtic goddess of the forge fire. She's red-hot and badass. There are tons of other goddesses associated with the coming of spring, but Imbolc (celebrated by Christians as St. Brigid's Day) is a holiday that celebrates the creative spark aspect of the goddess, the pilot light that rekindles the warmth of the world. It's thought of as a quickening holiday, where the fetal spring season begins to rouse itself to life. Brigid can be honored with offerings of milk and her incense smells of cinnamon. In addition to her forge duties, Brigid also presides over poetry, herbalism, and midwifery. Busy lady.

Candles are ritually important for Imbolc. Some traditions make a crown of tiny candles for a young person to wear during this ritual, and though I'm sure they do it safely, this practice rings all my fire alarm bells. When Christians celebrate Candlemas or St. Brigid's Day, people bring their candles to the church to be blessed.

Around this same time in the year, ancient Romans celebrated the festival of Lupercalia, aka Februa (from which we get the month's name), a time of purging or cleansing. The *lupe* in Lupercalia refers to wolves, specifically the she-wolf who, legend has it, nursed Romulus and Remus, the human twins who would go on to found the city of Rome. The holiday observance would be conducted by a young man, naked except for a pelt over his junk, running through the streets while playfully flogging anyone who hoped to conceive a child that year. Ladies would get naked to give him a better shot at it. It was probably all very hot, so clearly the Christian patriarchy felt the need to shut it down, box it up, and regurgitate it as St. Valentine's Day. Happy February. Here's your fucking chocolate.

Ostara

Spring equinox! So vernal. Like all the sabbats, this holiday has a billion names because it's a celebration of spring and renewal, and almost all cultures have a goddess of spring and renewal. Standing tall among them is Oestara, the Teutonic goddess of the spring, whose name is loaned, at least phonetically, to the modern Christian celebration of Easter. She is also said to be a variant of Ishtar (also called Astarte) of Mesopotamia, and Isis, the ancient Egyptian goddess. This is the time of year associated with rebirth and regeneration, and it's freaking fecund. Unlike Beltane, which is coming up next, the Ostara celebration primarily focuses on the vegetative fertility of the world, and not so much the fauna aspect of things. Nevertheless, rabbits, in their impressive procreative ability, are symbolic of this festival and are sacred to Oestara. Eggs are dyed and exchanged as gifts to bestow fertility and honor the goddess—all of which should be no shock to you, as evidenced by the extremely obvious corollaries of the Easter basket and the ubiquitous bunny.

Beltane

"Hooray, hooray, the first of May, outdoor fucking begins today!" That's the traditional May Day greeting at Enchantments. I thought it was traditional everywhere, but nope! It's just us pigs. Beltane is a cross-quarter day celebration of the height of spring. It's the source of the maypole, which you may have heard of, and its attendant folk dance, in which people circle around the tall phallic pole, each holding the end of a ribbon attached to the top. The dancers weave in and out, eventually entwining the whole thing. The ribbons represent each participant's wishes and intentions for the next season of the year, and in the end, all of these intentions are combined together in strength and power and pointed libidinously upward to diddle the sky.

The celebration of Beltane includes other flora/fauna fertility rituals, one of which inspired the juvenile little rhyme at the start of this section. The rites begin, naturally, with a bonfire. Witches love lighting shit on fire! Throughout the evening's festivity it is/was customary to sneak off with your sweetheart to go fertilize the fields with your sex.

FLYING

In its most literal interpretation, the Beltane fertility ritual would have us witches all going out to have reckless sex in the fields to inspire and be a part of the impregnation of the earth, hopefully resulting in good harvests come fall. But some witches would observe this more symbolically with the handy household phallus of their broomstick, "riding" it through the fields, aka leaping around like crazies, because the legend goes that your crops would grow as high as you could leap. Hot, right? Crops! Anyway, that's one version of the witches flying on broomsticks shtick.

While we're talking about brooms, we might as well mention "flying ointment." It's a trippy concoction of semi-poisonous/psychotropic plant essences extracted and fixed with some kind of fat or oil (my cannabis chefs out there know all about this process), used for seeing visions. Witches would anoint their brooms with the stuff, absorb the potent ointment through their labia, and fly! Even as I'm typing this in the past tense, I'm getting the distinct sensation that there are some witches out there at this very moment greasing up their broomsticks in a fallow field as if to say, "Old school, my ass!" Sadly, we don't do the ointment at the shop because we're not legally allowed to suggest that you ingest anything we make, even if it is only through your labia.

Midsummer

Midsummer is the summer solstice or thereabouts: a celebration of the longest day and shortest night. In the northernmost parts of the globe, the sun is visible for a full twenty-four hours at midsummer, the peak of the sun's triumphant journey. The way some Wiccans tie together the cycle of the seasons is through the story of the Oak and Holly Kings. It's a modern interpretation of various European myths and folk practices that dramatize the battle between light and dark, popularized in Wiccan circles by Stewart and Janet Farrar. The way I understand it, the Oak King and the Holly King are two different forms or phases of the God, or the male consort of the Goddess. In Wicca, the God and Goddess come in a billion different flavors, or aspects, while still maintaining their continuity. These two faces of the masculine divinity vie for the companionship of the Goddess, on whose fertility all life on Earth depends. In winter, when darkness reigns over the light, the Holly King is said to be taking his turn at the helm of the masculine part of creation. From Samhain (peak autumn) to Beltane (peak spring) the Holly King rules; the security of his position as king and his potency as consort to the Goddess/Queen peak at Yule (deck the halls with boughs of!), the longest night, and wane as the days grow longer. The Oak King gains power with the lengthening of the days and eventually overthrows the Holly King entirely at Beltane. The peak of his power is at midsummer, from which point, inevitably, the length of day wanes, as does his strength, and he dies along with all the grass and plants, except for holly. And round and round we go till we're dizzy. There are many variations of this story, of course. Plus there's a bit about how the Goddess is impregnated at a certain holiday and gives birth at another, but by the time I get all of that sorted it'll be . . .

Lammas

Lammas is also spelled Lughnasadh, named for the Celtic deity Lugh. He's a Lugh of all trades, this Lugh. He's sometimes associated with Mercury, but . . . I'm not sure that Mercury liked hard work as much as Lugh does. He's a craftsman, as well as patron of bards. I was enchanted when I came across a tale in which Lugh boasts of having the skills of a blacksmith, a wheelwright, and a bard, confirming that this story came from a time and place in which a bard was thought to possess skills of equal practical value as someone who knows how to make a vehicle or a weapon. Take me there! Maybe a good Lammas ritual visualization would be to imagine a world in which all of your best, most valuable skills were celebrated and meaningfully shared with your community, like the loaves and fishes. Actually, you might want to literally bake some bread and share it with people, because Lammas is a harvest celebration and is timed to occur around the point at which one would reap one's harvest of wheat, had they sown their seeds at Beltane when they were supposed to. (Tsk. I'm looking at you. I bet you didn't even sow!) The harvest season is a time to reflect on all of the non-wheat things we've cultivated during the previous months, how they've matured, and how to use it to nourish and sustain us as a community.

Holiday Reflections

So, what are we, a bunch of ancient farmers all of a sudden? And also, if Christianity is the opposite of Paganism, why should almost all of the feast days be observed in basically the same way? Who's sleeping with the Goddess and at what time of year? These are study questions to make sure you've been paying attention. There will be a test, or sabbat, every month and a half roughly, so bone up.

But there's one more thing . . .

ESBATS

Where the dates of the sabbats are responsive to the position and movement of the sun from one phase to another, the esbats are responsive to the phase and position of the moon. Sabbats are sunny solar occasions, celebrating, as we now know, the warmth and light of the sun as it revolves through the seasons. Esbats are lunar, and therefore take on a more mysterious shade.

MOON FACTS

I'm sure we all know a thing or two about the moon, but it'll help to be certain we're all on the same page with regard to its form and functions, the better to honor it.

- It takes twenty-eight days for the moon to complete a cycle through its phases. That's why the English word "month" is derived from the word "moon."

- Monday is named for the moon, so sometimes people will do their lunar-type magic on a Monday to get that extra layer of resonance.

- The lunar cycle is: new, waxing crescent, first quarter (half lit), waxing gibbous, full, waning gibbous, last quarter, waning crescent, new. "Waxing" means "getting bigger"; "waning" means "getting smaller."

To elaborate: The new moon is the time of the month when the moon is not visible in the sky, because the moon is between the earth and the sun, and we can only see the side that is not illuminated by the sun. Over the course of the month, the moon travels in its orbit around the earth and as it does so, we become able to see the side of the moon that is illuminated by the sun, a bit at a time. So by the time the moon has traveled about a quarter of the way around the earth, we see what is called the quarter moon. Then we see half of the illuminated side, and onward, until we eventually get a full view of the illuminated side, because the sun, earth, and moon are aligned again on the other side of the moon's orbital path. And so we'll continue going round and round until the sun explodes, I suppose.

Each month the full moon occurs in the zodiac sign *opposite* to the one the sun is in. For example, it's Aquarius season as I write this, and that means the full moon will be in the opposite sign, Leo. Isn't that a cool rule of thumb? Nette told me this, but when you think about it, it has to be right. When the moon is full it's across from the sun because that's why it's all illuminated. By the same coin, the new moon of each month is in the same sign as the sun is in at the time.

Esbats are where the real magic happens. At least that's what my friend Lord Wendy told me. He's a high priest, so he has a coven to convene with. He would know. Technically he could have an esbat any night of the week that's not a sabbat celebration. But you usually use the term to describe a ritual event that takes its occasion from the phase or position of the moon. They're often convened for the new and/or the full moon. In general, we use new moons to set intentions, sort of like sowing a seed that will grow with the moon throughout the month. The full moon illuminates things that would otherwise be hidden. That's a metaphor for divination if you ask me.

Esbats tend to take place at night. It just seems more logical to honor the moon when you can really get a look at her. Sometimes just standing under the moon and howling at it is esbat enough for me, but I'm a low-maintenance witch. Your esbat might be a crystal ball with partner dances, potions of absinthe, and a lunar dress code. If that's the case, invite me.

Chapter 7

PSYCHIC FRIEND NETWORKS, OR MAGICAL COLLABORATION

A lot of the things I've told you about so far are useful for the solitary witch, but there's tons of magic and witchcraft that you can access in a group setting or within the framework of an established religious tradition, or maybe via the sort of teacher-student relationship that ensures the passing on of a specific knowledge or lineage. At its best, a coven is a spiritual community or a mutual aid society of witches who hang out.

THE BUDDY SYSTEM

If a solitary witch is a coven of one, a two-person coven could be something like a working pair. In other words, two people whose energy is opposed in a productive way: opposites who have attracted each other, and who use that polarity of vibe as a way of generating creative magical energy. The communion between opposite, complementary forces is a kind of spiritual harmony that is ideally meant to be achieved within oneself and doesn't have to be expressed in magical pair work. But romantic couples, best friends, creative collaborators, or just two people with different approaches but the same energetic goal in mind can sometimes achieve things that one person might not be capable of on their own. It's often discussed as a male/female thing, but witches of all gender expressions can work effectively with anyone else whose energy is equal and opposite in some way. Some people prefer to collaborate with animal partners called familiars. The key point is to strike a dynamic circuit between two poles of opposite charge, like a battery, to raise energy to put into your magical intentions. I can always tell I'm approaching the right magical solution when Nette agrees with me. We approach situations from such different perspectives that when we reach the same conclusion, I feel like we must be on to something good.

FAQ: ARE THE CATS REAL?

We have a couple of black cats who live at the store. They're familiars, but please note that I mean familiar in the colloquial "pet with whom you share a psychic bond" sense of the term, not the arcane "animal-shaped devil vessel" sense. The  other day one of them took a bite out of my pizza, but not a little cat nibble— a bite like a man's. They're very sweet, they lie around on the counter and let all the crazy people pet them, and they hardly ever complain because they're patient creatures. But I lose patience entirely with the repetitive exchange that begins every seven minutes with someone opening the store's door and saying, "Oh my God! Is that a real cat?" No, it's not a real cat. It's a clever animatronic illusion. I still can't get over it! Are they real? *Yes!* They're actual living, breathing American shorthairs! I know I shouldn't take it so hard. It's a weird store. Maybe in some alternate universe we would have a set of incredibly lifelike artificial cats we could strew about in inconvenient places on the already crowded surfaces, but in this one we can only afford the living, breathing low-tech version.

Most of my coworkers would be perfectly happy to talk about the cats all day, but I just don't see where the conversation can go from there. Yes, there are two of them, and yes, they are brother and sister, but I can't imagine what difference it would make if there was a third cat you couldn't see and they were all second cousins once removed. Someone asked me the other day how old the cat is and I said nine, but really she's twelve. I don't know what effect this lie will have on my fate and the universe, but I'm willing to find out. I know I like cats. At least, I like the cats I know. What I hate is talking to strange humans about familiar cats.

I got my own cats from Enchantments back in the day. The old owners used to run a semi-accidental animal rescue operation out of the back room, and though it was long gone by the time I came around, that didn't stop people from dropping off orphaned cats on our doorstep every so often. There was a litter of three such orphans in the shop one day, and I was on the fence about taking one home. My coworker Michelle had found a home in Queens for one of them and was trying to convince me that two cats were actually easier to take care of than one, which somehow sounded rational at the time. Around that moment a very batshit customer came over to pet the kittens and tell them that she would take them home to meet her eleven other cats, and how she would name them Sabrina and Azriel, and before she could say another horrifying word, I adopted them. I called them LeRoy, after Bruce LeRoy, and Apollonia, after Apollo and after Prince's girlfriend in *Purple Rain*. But shit. Here I am talking to strangers about cats like I said I wouldn't. Let me stop.

SQUAD

Three to five witches with a similar goal in mind might convene to celebrate a moon or sabbat (see Chapter 6), or to collaborate on some sort of creative project of spiritual significance. I would count Mardi Gras krewes among this type of coven, although of course they might not describe themselves that way. I'm sorry, but any group of people who passionately devote so much time and creative energy to the goal of joy, beauty, excess, and shared pleasure are witches to me.

Every so often I'm lucky to be counted among an oven coven—a casual collection of kitchen witches, artists, writers, performers and friends who convene to create drinkable potions (usually cocktails) and other fanciful and experimental recipes from unique and bizarre ingredients. Think dragonfruit parfaits and honeycomb cakes. We meet up irregularly to share recipes, divvy up specialty ingredients that we buy in bulk, and work together to process (roast, peel, chop, grate) the magic ingredients.

But most of my experience of magical collaboration has been working at Enchantments. The best advantage of being an Enchantments witch isn't actually having access to all the books and materials a witch could hope for, though that is pretty good. The best resource by far is having one another to consult with. Everyone at Enchantments has some sort of specialty or some particular type of energy they lend to a situation, and we're in a constant conversation about how to approach our customers' questions and requests. You now know that there are a billion ways to tackle a spell, and it sometimes takes a coven to zero in on the most elegant magical solution. With so much up to interpretation, it is essential for me to bounce my magical logic off other people.

EVERYONE'S ALWAYS NICE ON THE INTERNET

When I tell people I work at Enchantments, they sometimes say, "Oh, I know that place. I heard they're really mean there." Hey, I'm nice. I'm hella nice, and I'm not even from California. But I'm only there once a week. Who knows which witches you'll get when you come in. Seriously, though, everyone I work with these days is genuinely nice, if not conventionally so. I think the thing about us that might rub people the wrong way is that while we aim to help, we don't necessarily aim to please. It's not your usual retail customer service model, but then Enchantments isn't your usual business. Sometimes people complain of being ignored; what they don't realize is that we're ignoring some customers because we're helping others to tease out their life issues and achieve their dreams. For tips. So yeah, sometimes we might tell you shit you don't want to hear, and TBH, sometimes we don't engage with people unless they have something specific to ask, because we need a break. Spending the day at the occult shop can be a lot, as you might imagine. Can you blame some of us for keeping firm boundaries with our customers? It's an intimate, strange, and narrow workspace full of weirdos and glitter and things on fire, where we practice unlicensed magical therapy while making custom wax carvings for whoever walks in off the street. Forgive us our occasional attitudes. Or don't. You can always shop online. Everyone's always nice on the internet.

COVEN

Some magical traditions are best explored in learned company, and as a part of a spiritual lineage. Like any other kind of craft, it helps to have experienced folks to guide you and peers to experiment with. In Wicca, the collective is called a *coven*. It's from the same Latin root as "convene" and "covenant." Traditionally, a coven consists of up to thirteen people, including a high priest and priestess. You'll have noticed that in Wicca, there's a great emphasis placed on the magical potential of the interplay between masculine and feminine energy (alternatively described as yin/yang, positive/negative, active/passive, projecting/receptive, Lenny/Squiggy). This is often represented by the balance between the high priest and priestess and, in the great rite, the simulation of sex (the knife phallus in the vag chalice), although you could totally do real sex in ritual and be in accordance with tradition, if that's how you and your coven get down. From what I hear, most modern Wiccan covens do not have real sex during ritual, though, so don't get your hopes up/get creeped out, as the case may be.

A lot of covens max out at thirteen people not because of superstition but because group dynamics are tricky enough at any number but just get unwieldy past a baker's dozen. So the Wiccans came up with a few ways of dealing with the overflow. The first is the hiving-off system, meant to mimic the way that when a bee population gets too large to be accommodated by its hive, another queen is cultivated. When mature, she flies off from the hive, taking some portion of the bee population with her to start anew elsewhere. The Wiccans do something similar, only it's people instead of bees, so the ins and outs of the process tend to be less interesting. In the course of writing this book I've come across a lot of accounts of intercoven politics, and *woof*—it's a drag. Suffice it to say, people are how we are, so having a mechanism for moving on from one another and doing your own thing when it's time sounds smart.

RELIGIONS OF THE DIASPORA

Many employees and people who come through Enchantments for ritual supplies are practitioners of New World religions based in African pantheons and spiritual traditions. To name a few, Santería, Vodou (Haiti), and Voodoo (southern United States) are adaptations of African religions and mystic practices that were brought with our enslaved ancestors, preserved, adapted to new lands and the dire needs of their circumstances, and hidden to varying degrees in the guise of Christian worship and iconography out of necessity.

Many of the deities of these different paths bear striking resemblances, like Elegua and Papa Legba, both keepers of the crossroads, tricksters, banishers of obstacles, and conduits between humans and divinity. Both Erzuli (Vodou) and Oshun (Santería) rule over the domains of love, lust, and sensuality, although their sacred stories and preferred colors, foods, and scents are different. While the variations between mystic traditions are vast, humans' spiritual needs remain stubbornly constant. Especially when one considers our enslaved ancestors, faced with no other option than to cobble together a means for spiritual survival on a strange continent under the most gruesome circumstances.

These gods are honored collectively among the spiritual community through ritual music, dance, and making offerings. Each of these traditions also involves some aspect of ritual possession of priests, initiated by the spirits being honored, a process referred to as being ridden by a spirit like a horse or *cheval.*

At the mention of possession, a certain segment of the population will inevitably fold their napkins and excuse themselves from the table. But please don't think that the sensationalized idea and practice of possession is unique to African diaspora spiritual expression. Wiccans and other Euro-based traditions have their own rituals of drawing down or inviting the God/dess to inhabit the body/mind of the priestess. But I suppose that any relinquishment of control over one's own body, spirit, or mind does ring some alarm bells for me and my ego, too. That's why these are traditions that involve a prescribed process of securing a spiritual support system (your godparents), initiation rites of purification, and a commitment to protect the sanctity of the group. That's why people who take part in these traditions often argue that the uninitiated shouldn't just dive in without first becoming a part of a trusting community that can support you as you do your deeper delving. Although that doesn't stop me from honoring these deities in other ways in my own practice.

CEREMONIAL MAGICK

Ordo Templi Orientis (Order of the Temple of the East, or Order of Oriental Templars) is an organization that is devoted to the practice of Western Ceremonial Magick, a collection of initiatory traditions that was popularized by a group called the Golden Dawn in early twentieth-century England. It's based in Renaissance-era magical practices passed down in *grimoires* (secret witchy diaries), ancient Egyptian practices, Kabbalah, Rosicrucianism—whatever they could get their hands on, really, plus a dash of their own wild-ass imaginations. Often fueled by a whole bunch of drugs, at least in the case of the patron asshole-saint of Ceremonial Magick, Aleister Crowley. Unfortunately, I can't tell you much about the many complex Escher-like interlocking levels of the Ceremonial Magick initiatory system because it would take all day. It is baroque, and frankly annoying. It seems as if it's designed to be impenetrable to outsiders! What gives? To be fair, a protective labyrinth is a primary function of many initiatory systems: it keeps the witch-hunters at bay. But Ordo Templi Orientis can keep its secrets. Its detail-oriented practices and complicated hierarchies are meant to appeal to a certain kind of person who is not me.

If you're itching to start a coven, my best advice at this point might be to get together with a few of your friends and try any of the spells and rituals that I've suggested that interest you. Choose a deity and build them an altar, throw a party in honor of that deity, and invite your friends! Or start a goddess group to share your research, and see if some of your fellows make good suggestions. There are some really amazing Internet-witches out there who have formed virtual magical communities through their work and dedication. Check them out! Support their work and then get inspired to do some work of your own.

Part Two

MAGICAL INTENTIONS

Chapter 8

GOOD HOUSEKEEPING, OR UNCROSSING, PROTECTION, AND BANISHING

Witchcraft is about noticing and engaging with the forces that are always operating in the world around us. It's about being sensitive to the . . . oh, fuck it, I'm just gonna go ahead and say "vibes" again for lack of a better term. Truly, I've tried to find one, but "vibes" is the most precise. I'm not talking about cultivating some sort of extrasensory perception; I'm simply encouraging you to fully employ the senses you already have to be a more active participant in your own life.

Grant Morrison calls this state of awareness Magical Consciousness in his "Pop Magic!" essay, which I've already mentioned, and which, not incidentally, inspired me to write this book.

> *Magical consciousness is a way of experiencing*
> *and participating with the local environment in a*

heightened, significant manner, similar to the ef-
fects of some drug trips . . . near death experiences,
etc. . . . This is the state in which tea leaves are
read, curses are cast, goals are scored, poems are
written.

In practice, this could be as simple and revolutionary a practice as giving your intuitive self the credit it deserves for quietly steering you away from danger and toward your goals. Developing a practice of checking in occasionally with that inner voice can help it grow louder and even more helpful.

So, how do you let your intuitive self know that you're listening? By heeding her warnings and following her indications. If you're in a situation that feels weird, that's because it *is* weird. Even if it's not a full-on fight-or-flight scenario, honor that little voice by acknowledging that what you feel is real. If you get the feeling that you shouldn't trust someone, it's because you shouldn't. If the person you want to date seems uninterested, it's because they are. You don't need to be psychic to figure out these things, but people go to psychics to figure out these things every day. And they pay so much money for it. Morrison suggests a few additional experiments or exercises to strengthen these psychic muscles:

Relax, go for a walk and interpret everything you
see on the way as a message from the Infinite to
you. Watch for patterns in the flight of birds. Make
oracular sentences from the letters on car number
plates. . . . Pay attention to noises on the streets,
graffiti sigils, voices cut into rapid, almost sublim-
inal commands and pleas. Listen between the lines.

Walk as far and for as long as you feel comfortable in this open state. The more aimless, the more you walk for the pleasure of pure experience, the further into magical consciousness you will be immersed.

I love cruising around town in this state of readiness for magic. But if you want to be able to enjoy your newfound psychic openness, you'll have to institute some protective boundaries and learn methods of cleansing so that you're not out there blowing in the cosmic breeze like a dirty old windsock. You could go crazy leaving yourself open to whatever energies just happen to be floating by. You need to take preventative measures. This is kind of like wearing a raincoat over your aura, so you can shake off any clingy feelings that you catch from the people you interact with: for example, shame from someone's sideways glance on the train, or an extreme case of the willies caught off someone who comes into your place of work claiming to be possessed and making strange dagger eyes and twitching because, he says, the demon inside of him resists his attempt to rid himself of it. It happens. And what can you say but, "Hi! Can I help you?" Nonononononono, I can't help you. Of course I can't help you, I'm not an exorcist. To be totally honest, I've never even seen *The Exorcist.* But when I'm not keeping up a firm sense of the boundaries of my mental and emotional space, someone acting that weird, in that context, could rattle me.

NEEDLE PEOPLE PART 1

I've seen this dude since. He's not possessed, just so, so strange. And probably in pain. I could understand that much. He came in on my first day back at the store after a fifteen-year absence, and I felt trapped behind the sticky, ancient cash register, trying to face this poor guy in his tattered Hot Topic gothery, as he refused all of my helpful suggestions. He was sure that Uncrossing, Banishing, and Devil-Be-Gone were all too weak for his special possession problem. And now that I think of it, he was right. That guy needs help from a special kind of specialist. I managed to dispatch him kindly and without taking any of his money. But he still comes in every now and again to ask for some randomly disquieting item. Last time it was black needles, whatever the hell that is.

"Do you have black needles?"

"You mean, like for sewing? But black?" we asked him.

And he was like, "Needles? Black needles?" All pale.

So we were like, "Porcupine quills? No? Like a needle painted black? Why don't you paint a needle black?"

Just some disturbed, disturbing kid who comes and goes in five minutes, like a midafternoon thunderstorm. But there it hangs in my mind, because I'm sensitive to stuff, and I had forgotten that day to take a moment to declare my intention of insulating myself from the creeper vibes of my fellow man.

That's why maintenance is a big part of a witch's work. Take precautions. You could also call it magical hygiene or psychic self-defense, but it's very necessary, like Salt-N-Pepa. There are so many different ways of approaching the idea that it goes by a few different names, but I'll do my best to give some simple ways to protect yourself from free-floating negativity, as well as methods for clearing any bummer vibes that may have already accumulated.

CRYSTALS

If you're into crystals, you're in luck, because quite a few of them can be worn or carried to help protect your home, physical safety, or psychic space. I'll list some prime examples below.

- Black tourmaline. This crystal is said to absorb negativity when carried or worn. It's pretty rad-looking, both matte and shiny at the same time in its natural form, and it's not particularly expensive or hard to find. I might suggest this as a helpful cubicle crystal for a workplace toxicity.

- Smoky quartz. Another inexpensive and easy-to-find crystal, smoky quartz is said to be a grounding influence, helpful in dispelling negative emotions. Carrying a smoky quartz can help to stabilize the emotions—particularly useful for those of us who have trouble keeping our feet firmly planted.

- Tigereye. Roman soldiers were known to have carried amulets of tigereye into battle, for physical protection and to promote the courage necessary to rise up to the challenge of their rivals. Now that I think of it, I can't imagine a better incantation for a charging ritual for a tigereye than getting pumped listening to

Survivor's "Eye of the Tiger" with the stone in your hand. God, now I wanna try it.

- Pumice. With its uniquely porous surface, pumice is supposed to absorb negative energy like a sponge. A simple banishing ritual is to visualize whatever energy you want to be rid of flowing from your hand into the stone, and then chucking it into a body of water and never looking back. The same process can be performed with any other receptive stone, but the porousness of pumice makes it particularly sympathetic.

UNCROSSING

Meet your new best friend. Uncrossing: the Mr. Clean of magic spells. It's a clearance of negative energy, a removal of blockages, a dispersal of icky vibes, and a shedding of all the dusty old spiritual and emotional junk that sometimes sticks to a body. Any body, really. But I would wager especially to the bodies of those people who give a shit about this sort of thing. People who concern themselves with their own emotional or spiritual life will have noticed that there are moments when you feel unbalanced, or just . . . off somehow. Writers call it "blocked," nerds call it "stymied," witches say "crossed," "jinxed," "cursed," or "hexed." Those are high-drama words for slipping into some degree of a slump. At Enchantments, we prefer to talk about this condition in its inverse by offering Uncrossing, Unjinxing, Unhexing, et cetera. Why? Because walking around proclaiming oneself cursed is a sure way to make things seem worse.

The idea behind uncrossing is that it's a wiping clean of your slate, magically speaking. It's a shake of your Etch A Sketch. Wait, I have more! We have to explain and reexplain this concept to people all day long at Enchantments, so we're constantly accumulating metaphors. Spiritual Drano! That's a favorite of mine. But for real, the idea is to clear away anything that's not serving you, any stumbling blocks in your path, or anything unimportant or distracting.

MORE MAGICAL CHORES

You've heard this from me before, but the first step in any uncrossing spell is to clean your filthy apartment. If you feel like things are falling down around you, make sure that you don't actually have things falling down around you. And if you're sitting there all smug, like, "My place is clean. I make my bed every day, blah blah blah," then you can shut up. You think you're so special. I'll get to you later. I'm talking to the rest of us.

Ritual cleansing is a lot like regular cleaning, only ritual cleansing takes even more attention, because you're after the residue that you can't see. Your attentive gaze in each corner, under the couch, and on top of the cabinets is in itself a cleaning agent. Once you mop your floor the normal way, fill a bucket with diluted Florida water, which, as you might remember from Chapter 1, is an inexpensive cologne splash that's available at your nearest bodega or botánica, or on the internet if you don't have any such nearby. It smells like a tutti-frutti mixture of all the flowers in the whole world with alcohol. I like it, but if that's not your style, don't worry. There are lots of ways to cleanse your space. You probably never wondered why Mr. Clean smells like lemons, or why there's pine in Pine-Sol. But if you did, wonder no more, because lemon and pine are two of the many fresh, bright, astringent smells that are used magically for cleansing and uncrossing. So what's the difference between ritual cleaning and just regular boring cleaning? you might ask. Not much! The real difference is the perspective you take on the practice. Cleaning is already a powerful ritual. The question here isn't how to make cleaning your house magical, but how to use the little rituals you already have in your daily life to greater spiritual effect. Any cleaning can be ritual cleaning if you intend it to be. Ever kiss a fallen morsel of food up to God? Ever give yourself a circle-circle-dot-dot cootie shot? That's ritual cleansing. Any bath can become a ritual bath. Scrub awhile at the surface of any of your mundane activities and associations, and you might notice that you've been performing magic all along.

Some of the most basic household items can be used intentionally for cleansing beyond the literal. My favorite power combo for cleansing is a simple salt and lemon scrub that I use in the shower to rid myself of any leftover icky vibes from, for instance, a particularly intense day of interacting with . . . I'll call them "needle people." I cut the lemon in half, cover the cut surface with salt, and give myself a scrub from the top of my head down, squeezing the lemon as I go. I follow that up with a bracing cold-water rinse. Salt water and lemon water are among the most highly recommended cleaning agents for ritual items, crystals, jewelry, or anything you use for magic. I like to sprinkle a witch hazel solution that you can get at the drugstore over myself for a quicker energetic refreshment when I don't have time for a whole bath or shower, but other people might use a splash of orange water, holy water, or any number of other ritual colognes to serve the same purpose.

A good way to approach an uncrossing is with a candle spell. As I mentioned in Chapter 3, our standard practice at Enchantments is to offer uncrossing to anyone who comes in and takes a deep breath when you ask them what they want a candle for, and then goes on to say, "Oh, a lot of things," or "Oh my God, where to begin?" or "Can I do it for a bunch of stuff?" If you don't know what you want from a magical intention candle, it can't really do anything for you, so an uncrossing candle is the way to go. Clarity of vision is key when you're attempting to envision the best, most fulfilling life for yourself and, if we're doing this thing right, for all living things. In the interest of a better world, it's on each of us to get our own shit together so it doesn't distract us so much from the larger things at hand.

The typical uncrossing candle bears a symbol that looks like a crossroads: one line runs from the top of the candle to the bottom, and another runs through the middle. Where the lines intersect, you make a circle that represents the person working the spell standing at a crossroads. That's the visualization that is usually suggested with uncrossing: imagine yourself at the center of a crossroads, with clear paths leading toward and away from you in each direction.

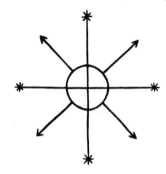

This symbol is typically carved on a white candle (see Chapter 2, on colors). When I say carve, I don't mean anything fancy. Draw in the wax with some kind of pointed tool. I use a Swedish pocket knife with a wooden handle. It's a cute, sporty $20 model, because I'm worth it. And because the blade is only sharp on one side, and it comes to a point that's about the right width to carve a nice clear moat in the wax, the right depth to hold on to the oil and glitter or herbs I plan to work into the design. The elaborateness of the seal varies depending on the size of the candle, but they all generally strike that same crossroads pose. If you have a white candle but it's stuck in the glass, no problem. Get yourself a sacred Sharpie and get to work drawing the same kind of thing on the glass. Blue is a nice complementary color to add to your intention, because, as you know, blue is used for calming, peacefulness, and protection. I made an uncrossing candle for a friend once with a bodega candle and some tubes of silver glitter glue I got at the dollar store (because silver is useful for neutralizing and balancing). In magic as in life, sometimes you gotta improvise. Maybe all the time.

Some people come back after an uncrossing candle to say things to the effect of, "Hey, so after I burned that candle, I lost my job and my boyfriend moved out, but then I ran into an old friend from years ago and we're dating now and I'm going back to school, and I'm really happy, and . . . I guess it worked?" Yes, honey. It worked. If your job and relationship weren't serving you, then you needed to make space for the things that *would* serve you. Nette always talks about how uncrossing is an act of faith, because you trust in the universe, or whatever it is that you trust in, to fill the space you're creating with whatever it is that you really need.

But clearing the space can be difficult. Sometimes it seems easier to grasp whatever's holding you back than to have to deal with the uncertainty of empty hands. It's that Puritan fundamentalism that our country was built on, rearing its head with that bird-in-the-hand shit. I don't buy it. You'll never know if the bird in your hand is better than those two in the bush over there, unless you try to catch them. And even if you hold on real tight to that one bird you've got, you'll still die like the rest of us, only not knowing. I bet those two birds are the best fucking birds ever, over there in that green, green grass. Imma go get 'em.

NEEDLE PEOPLE PART 2

What is it about needles? Another, um, needle-oriented customer came to the back desk at the shop to ask for a spell to help her find more clarity in her life. Her way of easing into polite conversation as we worked was this, apropos of nothing: "I have a needle in my head! No, really, it's true. It happened when I was a baby. It used to happen all the time during the turn of the last century, because women were always sewing and darning even when they had a baby in their lap, and every so often a needle would fall point down on a baby's soft spot and embed itself in the brain somewhere. *I'm serious.* And I have one. My mom says she has no idea how it got there, but I was born in Russia, so . . . maybe that's why." What do you say to that? "Mmm-hmmm"? Or maybe "Oh!" or "Okaaay" or any other noncommittal syllable dragged out to express dubiousness but an unwillingness to argue the point? She was all right, but she needed some uncrossing. And an unneedling, if at all possible.

PROTECTIVE MAGIC

According to Scott Cunningham (see Chapter 4), protective magic ranks highest among magical categories in terms of the number of herbs and spells associated with the intention. A magical item intended for the specific purpose of protecting the bearer from harm is called an *amulet*, not to be confused with a *talisman*, which is an item that can either ward off harm or draw some other kind of energy. (The two are easily confused because that's a fussy distinction.) Even avowedly nonreligious people make use of amulets in their lives. The urge to protect ourselves and our loved ones is so strong that most people at one time or another feel compelled to ritualize that intention by charging amulets with that protective wish, to make it tangible and portable. Maybe you have a St. Christopher medal, or a pentacle, or Star of David, or that Italian horn, for just such a purpose.

As far as my mother is concerned, whenever I travel beyond the tri-state area, I might as well be rappelling off the side of a cliff at the edge of the world. As soon as I leave the spaces that she has mapped out mentally from her personal experiences, I am in terra incognita, like thar be monsters thar. I can understand the feeling. My mind definitely gives me the option to go there when the people I love feel far beyond my ability to protect them. But then, if I'm lucky, I remember that they're beyond my control at all times, even when in more seemingly predictable circumstances. The options remain to freak out or not to freak out. Sometimes we can confuse praying and hoping for the safety of our loved ones with focused visualization of all the horrible things that can happen in life. It's a thin line for some of us, so it's important to stay on the protective visualization side of things and not fall into the anxiety trap.

The kind of care that parents and nurturers provide to the people and beings they care for is, in fact, magical: it is the invisible impulses that sustain life! Soon after I became a mom, I wondered why I hadn't felt the impulse to do any protective magic for the baby. Then I realized that everything I do is protective magic for the baby. There's a whole new channel in my brain, and it's a constant stream of subconscious protective magic for my child. J. K. Rowling didn't lie! Harry Potter's mom set that whole chain of events into motion with the most powerful spell in the whole fictional universe, and it didn't have a name or a Latinate incantation, but it beat every other spell in the book.

My favorite kind of protective magic is the psychic blue bubble meditation that I mentioned in Chapter 2. It's even more portable than a tiny amulet because it's all in your head! Very convenient packaging! But if you're looking for something tangible, I'm going to give you a formula from Herman Slater's *Magickal Formulary*, one of the foundational texts of the shop. Don't tell anybody about it. You must take a sacred oath of secrecy. But before you get too excited, you'll find that the formulas don't always specify the origin of the spell, the intended amounts, or even the form (leaf, root, oil) the listed ingredients are meant to take. It's up to each witch to determine whether to blend it as an oil or incense, and then to somehow know when it smells and feels just right for what it's meant to do. That's why magic is referred to as an art or a craft. You have to bring all of your senses to your magical work; you have to get your hands dirty and be willing to mess up sometimes.

But do try! If you can't get your hands on some of these ingredients, that's cool. Tinkering around with spells can be so much fun, and if you don't have a whole magickal apothecary at your disposal, I'll model how to substitute ingredients you don't have or don't like so you won't be held back from experimentation for lack of storax or benzoin. (That was a trick example! Benzoin and storax are the same thing.) It's also a great opportunity for you to grab your witches' herbal or go online to do your own research on magical substitutions.

PEACEFUL HOME

Lemon

Rose

Lilac

This is an old Hoodoo blend. It's usually made as a powder that you sprinkle around the perimeter of your home as a way of drawing a circle of protection, and to ensure a calm and harmonious vibe within its boundary. If you want to blend a powder, you can use a base of arrowroot or any other natural powder that you might use on your skin. Grind up dried roses, lilac blossoms, and lemon peel in a mortar and pestle or coffee grinder, and add the mixture to your base, along with maybe some drops of essential oil of the same scents. While you're blending and sniffing and balancing your spell, add your vision of a peaceful home to the mix. The same blend could be helpful to clear the air after an argument by adding a bit of the essential oil of each ingredient to a diffuser. Or put a few drops in the bath for a peaceful soak.

So simple! But wait. If I'm honest, I kind of hate lilac. I mean, it's lovely IRL, in the spring, on a bush, but in its concentrated form it can be cloying, and it's almost impossible to get as an essential oil because the delicate little blossoms don't really lend themselves to the distillation process. So you have to get a fragrance oil and who knows the quality, blah blah blah. I think I'm better off using a substitute.

When looking for substitutes, a good place to start is by identifying the planet and element that the original ingredient is associated with. My herbal says that lilac is counted on team Venus, in the water division, so let's scan the list of Venus herbs for alternative purple flowers. Violet: purple, cloying, associated with Venus . . . promising! Looking *that* up, I see that it's also water, and also used to promote peace in the home. Damn! I got lucky! It's got the right vibe, plus extra points for flair.

SANCTIFYING SPACE

Like declaring the bottom stair "base" in tag, most rituals and spells employ some kind of outline—a drawing of a boundary around the safe space where the ritual is to take place. Think of it like metaphorically peeing in a circle around the area that is henceforth to be considered ritual space. Obvi, most temples and churches are similarly cordoned off, only with walls and fences that mark where the ritual spaces begin and end. But since witches, magicians, or whatever you magical kids are calling yourselves don't often have or want permanent, designated sanctified space, the boundaries of ritual become a bit more of an abstract concept, necessitating the casting of a circle. Some Pagan groups begin all of their magical meetings (sabbats and esbats; see Chapter 6) with a casting of the circle. Like all things, the exact character of the ritual would be up to you and your friends, if you practice in a group. Sometimes the circle is drawn on the ground or floor; other times the circle is formed by the people in it. The leader, or high priest or priestess, will often call the group to order by calling on the protection of the four directions and the spiritual concepts that your group relates to each. Some would consider this protective shielding magic *banishing*, but other traditions might call it an *invocation*, as in invoking the protection of the forces that you're honoring. I don't personally care to call it one thing or another, but I practice alone, so I don't have to. Me, I like to sanctify my ritual space, be it outdoors or my bathroom, with fragrant smoke, like sweetgrass or sandalwood. It's just another way of declaring, "Hey, see this area here? Bounded by these walls, the earth below, the sky above, and the scented air that fills the space in between? This space is dedicated to a ritual purpose!"

HAUNTING

A lot of people think their house is haunted. A friend asked recently if I could help his roommate, who kept waking up with mysterious scratches (from a ghost?). Another friend's shelves kept falling out of the walls (because of ghosts?). I don't doubt their sincerity, but no matter what genus of bump in the night you're experiencing, this book can't tell you whether or not your house is haunted. Apparently I can't even tell if *my* house is haunted.

I assumed that Enchantments would feel kind of creepy if you were there alone at night, but Nette slept there once and told me it felt surprisingly normal. Then Nette stayed over at my place with my cat while I was out of town and told me I had some nerve asking about the store given the haunted-ass house that I live in. I was surprised until she figured out that at least one of the spirits was a cat, and the others were probably just my own beloved dead, hanging out around my home for fun. And then I was like, "Oh! You mean them!" I keep an altar to my recent ancestors, hold on to their heirlooms, and think of them often. So if that's a kind of haunting, I'll take it.

As much as I enjoy the idea of living and moving among the spirits of my grandparents, I don't pretend to know what happens after we die. How could I know something like that? Would you believe someone who said that they did? And also: who cares? But somehow that doesn't stop me from envisioning my own dead walking with me like the illest entourage, backing me up when I need backing up. It feels good and it makes me stronger. Is that their spirits lending me their strength? Yes. No. Maybe. I fail to see the difference between an active relationship with the memory of someone and being guided by their spirit. I wouldn't doubt the sincerity of anyone who did see an essential difference between those concepts, but to me they fold neatly into each other, coexisting in my little Swiss army knife of esoteric tools that I use to make my life feel like my own, to find myself within a lineage, and to feel grateful for the responsibility to make the most of it.

BANISHING

If you're still feeling haunted and it doesn't feel like friendly ancestors, and it doesn't seem like uncrossing and protective magic are doing the trick, then maybe you'll want to do a banishing ritual.

I don't like to encourage customers at the shop to describe their ghosties in detail for a few reasons, chief among them that it's really boring. Even if it's a really vibrant ghost that does all sorts of knocking over of things and poltergeisty shit, I still don't want to hear about it at any great length. It's like listening to a stranger's dream. I know I'm not being nice, but I'm excusing myself because focusing your attention on whatever's vexing you is out of step with the intention of banishing. By that I mean, try not to devote too much time and energy to analyzing whatever negative-feeling manifestation you might find in your home. I'm not saying there's nothing there to analyze. I'm just saying that our first job in removing it is finding a way to reclaim the energy we might otherwise use in being so fucking interested in it, whatever *it* may be!

Banishing sounds terribly serious, but it's actually fun. No, really. People never believe me the first time I say that, and there *are* many formulas for banishing incense and potions, but the most effective banishing rituals involve fun and joy. Maybe it sounds something shy of witchy, but when you really think about it, of all the stereotypes about witches—like being evil or having prominent nose warts—the cackling is actually a real thing. It's not often that the type of laughter emitted by a specific type of person is distinctive enough to warrant its own terminology, but the laughter of witches does in fact possess a quality of anarchic power that is equaled only by the muaahaahaha of villains and the hilarity of the manic. Many witches find themselves at one time or another consigned to one or both of those categories.

The energy of sincere mirth drives away, or banishes, evil. If you feel like you need to get rid of a persistent funky energy, your laughter, light, and pleasure are among your most valuable magical tools. Do a cleansing ritual, or maybe just a tidying-up ritual, in your previously haunted space, and then throw a party in there! Cook a meal, have a drink, smoke a joint! Laughter in the face of what frightens you is the most effective form of banishing. The sound of our stubborn, enduring joy at being alive is apparently repulsive to the gremlin set, so do your best to whoop it up.

SUGGESTED READING

Draja Mickaharic, *Spiritual Cleansing* (Weiser, 2012)

Herman Slater, ed., *The Magickal Formulary* (Magickal Childe, 1981)

Chapter 9

EVERYONE'S KIND OF STUPID ABOUT LOVE, OR ATTRACTION MAGIC

Your task is not to seek for love, but merely to seek and find all the barriers within yourself that you have built against it.

—Rumi

Can you believe I just quoted Rumi? What nerve! Who am I, Oprah? What is this, yoga? I've finally gone too far. But just because I had the chutzpah to bust out the ancient Persian mystic poetry doesn't mean you don't have to reckon with the realness of my Rumi quote, because that's what the love chapter of this book is all about. If you're here for the secret to getting cute Jane or hot Johnny to be obsessed with you, you're probably not going to like what I have to say: your idea is a bad idea, and your plan is a bad plan. It's an eminently doable sort of magic but also some of the most fuck-up-able. I'll outline some better ideas and plans so that you can get what you actually want, which, it turns out, is not just more attention from the person who chooses not to spend their attention on you. This is a hard truth that a lot of us end up banging our heads against again and again, like a locker door in a 1980s rom-com, but that's okay. We're all burdened with juvenile-flavored fantasy when it comes to love and romance; there have been a lot of movies, you guys! So much bullshit messaging coming through and gumming up the works.

As with all intentions, before starting any love magic, it's essential to figure out a few concrete things that you actually want. Maybe you want someone who enjoys long walks on the beaches and makes you laugh. Whatever those things are, make your points specific enough to weed out some segment of the population. Unfortunately, beach walking and laughter are horrible examples, because you'd have to be a philistine not to appreciate the liminal majesty of the seashore, and every dumbass thinks they're funny. Think of better examples than I did! That's your job. Maybe it's an employed, independent person who loves birdwatching as much as you do, or a Burning Man man who likes anchovies on his pizza. Build your perfect mate, specific to you, made not of the things you think you should want but of what really and truly does it for you.

Being attractive to the people you want to attract is one thing, and it's a readily doable kind of magic. People have devoted so much time and energy to the pursuit that it's a well-researched category. Being clear about whom and what you want to attract and keep is a whole other beast, and a far trickier one to figure out, because a lot of us have a complicated relationship with our self-worth and think that we should settle for something at our own expense. Have you ever listened to Mariah Carey's "Vision of Love"? I mean, really listened, because it's so exceedingly simple but so super-deep you don't even know. I want someone to use it as the incantation for a love spell, because it's a perfect literal explanation of the spell process, but I'm afraid that if I print the lyrics here Mimi will sue me, so suffice it to say that she had a clear mental picture of love, and she prayed through the night soooooo faithfully . . . anyway, you get it. The song even contains a short list of important qualities in a lover, including kindness (probably the most important one of all), and outlines the process of visualizing, holding faith, and receiving your blessings with gratitude. Thank you, Mimi.

Where was I? I think I was saying you gotta make a list. You may also want to note a few key points that people always forget, like availability and proximity, because what if you meet someone who ticks all the boxes, but they're already attached in a way that doesn't work for you, or they're available and interested but a thousand miles away? That's the lesson of misguided love magic: it's not that it doesn't work, it's just that when it does, *you get what you want, but you don't really want what you get.*

Lemme break it down for you further, because this is important. There are a few different approaches to love magic. That's an understatement. There are endless approaches to love magic, but I'm going to generalize and say that there's the pushy kind and the pully kind.

The pushy kind is, true to its name, a very rude (some would say unethical) way to go about things. When people come into the shop hoping to bring back someone who has chosen of their own free will to leave a relationship, I consider that pretty pushy. We can almost always talk people out of taking this approach to relationship "mending," sometimes just by casually offering alternatives and other times by explaining, repeatedly, that the cost of interfering with another person's will is real and corrosive. You give up your ability to be satisfied. The most obvious sign that manipulative love magic doesn't work is that people who do it are doing it all the damn time. Real love makes and remakes itself. Manipulation requires constant maintenance.

Sometimes, even when I've explained that to a customer, they still want that shit. And depending on how they approach the employee, they might get what they want. We try to dissuade people from manipulative magic whenever possible and refuse service whenever we want to. We're under no obligation to help people be nasty. All of my favorite workspaces strictly adhere to a "fuck outta here" policy. I've met a lot of magical creeps in the line of duty, and it really shows. Like in their faces. Like they're lit up by an ugly slant of light. We're very, very happy to lose the business of people who don't listen to reason. And while we're being sassy, I'll just take this opportunity to say:

YOU SHOULD PROBABLY JUST BREAK UP WITH HIM

"But I love him" is among my least favorite phrases in the English language. It's only employed to excuse letting someone shit all over you and going back for more, even when it causes you all kinds of pain and strife, and calling that *love*. And even if that *is* love, you can find that kind of love anywhere. Why hang on? Have faith that whatever or whoever you're looking for will be a true fit, not something that only hangs right if you stand back and squint. This lady came into the shop recently, and when I offered my help, she said, "I think I want to break up with my fiancé. So I guess I need a candle for, like, clarity or something." I said, "Well, you just walked into a store and told a strange witch that you wanted to break up with your fiancé. You sound pretty clear to me. Why don't you just go do it?" She left. I don't think she bought anything, but she got what she needed: permission from some external source of (very dubious) moral authority. So I hereby grant you, too—whoever needs to read this right now—express permission to break up with whoever and whatever isn't serving your needs. Really. Make room in your life for something better. There may be scarcity in the world, and in life, but the best love magic doesn't deal in hoarding tactics. That's just not how it's played. You can't be stingy with love. (You'll hear the same thing from me when it comes to money magic in Chapter 10.) You can't expect an outpouring of riches from the heavens when you don't engage in free exchange. This may sound kind of stupid, but this is love we're talking about. Everyone's kind of stupid about love.

So that's why, blessedly, there's the pully kind! I'm so excited to tell you about it, and I'm patting myself on the back for my new nomenclature! It's also known as love drawing, attraction, glamour, animal magnetism—you know what the hell I'm talking about, so call it whatever you want. There are a billion zillion different styles and flavors of it because people have holes and pegs that come in all shapes and sizes. Imagine me making rude hand gestures right now to illustrate. This magic is about cultivating your own most lovable qualities and weaponizing them, lovingly, toward the end of attracting an energy that's complementary to your own. A lot of Wiccans work with the concept of polarity, or the necessity in life and magic of opposing charges to generate the energy needed to create something new. Because of this, many Wiccans work in pairs (often male/female pairs) to highlight the polarity and generate psychic energy between these poles, like a battery, all of which—stay with me here—is a metaphor for the congress between the God (or resonant archetype of active, fiery, potent qualities) and the Goddess (or resonant archetype of receptive, generative, fluid qualities), whose love affair is metaphorically played out in the cycles of fertility in the natural world (see the story of the Oak and Holly Kings in Chapter 6). The love magic approach that I tend to recommend involves choosing one of the roles in this story and trying it on as you would a costume. The trick is to become, for a time, the aspect of the God or the Goddess that most reminds you of yourself at your very best, your very most adorable.

LADY OF LARGEST HEART

Inanna is the ancient Sumerian goddess of love, sex, and making babies, with a touch of the warrior thrown in for good measure. One of the oldest documented goddesses in existence, she came into being as a fertility goddess (in the vegetative sense). Circa 2250 BCE, Enheduanna, an influential poet-priestess, proclaimed Inanna to be as one with another love and battle goddess of the time, Ishtar. In her femme fatale form, Inanna went on to inspire the Greek seductress Aphrodite and the Roman Venus (goddess and planet), while in her more butch incarnations, parts of her mythos were incorporated into that of Athena Nike, battle strategist. When depicted in this warlike aspect, she is often astride a lion, as if to say, "I'm so fierce, I use the king of beasts like you would use a yellow cab." Inanna is unambiguously described as independent and ambitious. Merging with Ishtar via Enheduanna was definitely a boss move. With their powers combined, Inanna/Ishtar became the hottest, most powerful goddess out there, due in no small part to the fact that Enheduanna's poetry in her honor is the first work of literature to bear the author's name. It seems Inanna's example inspired Enheduanna to make some sexy, badass, boss moves of her own.

When I talk about trying on a role, I mean trying it in your mind. I know research doesn't sound very sexy to some of us, but learning the attributes, attitudes, and preferences of a deity provides you with a new set of indicators to remind you of your intention. For instance, if you know that Oshun loves pumpkins, shiny golden sparkly things, rivers, yellow flowers, and champagne, as you go through your day you can allow any instance of any of those things to remind you of her, and of the alluring parts of you that follow in her cosmic example.

I CALL HER AFRO-DITE

Oshun. She's the *orisha* (goddess of Yoruba extraction) of sensual love and abundance and round brown body gorgeousness, and we're BFFs. Beyoncé took her shape in the "Hold Up" video in *Lemonade*, killing the whole game in billowing gold and joyfully wrecking heads. Or the queen Ms. RiRi, at the Met Gala in her ten feet of yellow train looking like the canary that ate the canary, enchanting, tapping directly into our innate hedonistic craving for luxe sweetness, to be bathed by a tongue of honey. Oshun is the bubbles in the champagne.

Another way to get into the part is to wear the scents associated with the sexy archetype that you're trying on. I listed a few usual suspects below, but you should think of the internet as your very own exhaustive list. Do some research on love deities and their sacred scents. I humbly suggest that you might want to start by looking for archetypes from your own cultural background(s). You don't have to stop there, but I'm a firm believer in the idea that the magic you need is always close to hand.

We make blended oils to honor these sexy queens at Enchantments—lots of places do—but you can get the job done with any one of the scents in isolation:

- To honor Aphrodite (Miss Venus if you're Roman), try rose, orris, jasmine, or ylang-ylang.
- To get into the Oshun mood, you might try cinnamon, sandalwood, or star anise.
- Freya from the Norse pantheon and Erzulie from Vodou are both partial to strawberry.
- Egyptian musk for Cleopatra, apple blossom for Eve . . . we could go on like this forever.

Pick a god or goddess and use their sublime qualities to lure your equal opposite. Which brings us to the sex talk.

The sex talk! It shouldn't take long. It's not such a talky department, it's more of a do-ey department. I should really just hand you over to Nette, because astrologically my Mars and my Venus are in Pisces (the planets of lust and love in the sign of dreams and illusion), which means I can't separate sex and love for shit. My emotions are my strength, so to go into a situation, any situation, with my emotions tied behind my back feels like putting myself unnecessarily at a disadvantage. Nette, on the other hand, has Mars in Aquarius (group activities) and Venus in Sagittarius (big party). When I read that line to Nette she got *very excited* thinking about my hands being tied behind my back. Note the distinction.

When we're talking about modern witchcraft culture and Old World European pre-Christian culture, two cultures whose every rite and ritual are in some way concerned with a phase or aspect of a cycle of fertility, there's gonna be, um, some adult content in that conversation. Practicing in a Wiccan coven isn't really a path for the prudish. Some, not all, covens practice their rituals *skyclad*, which is witchy jargon for naked. There's plenty of openly sexual symbolism built into the liturgies (as opposed to the sublimated sexual symbolism you'll find in other religions' rituals).

At Enchantments we engage in more than our share of NSFW talk in our workplace—nothing untoward, just anatomically correct and constant. I mean, we have penises and vaginas in the form of candles strewn all over the place. Or are they candles in the form of penises and vaginas? Who's to say? But we have them in three colors. I already told you about Filthy Sheets (see Chapter 2), but a good half of the magical recipes in our recipe Rolodex are for sexual or romantic attraction. It's interesting to be in a position where on a normal workday you collude with strangers on the best way to get them laid. From a certain vantage, the witches of Enchantments have been the secret wing people to a small but sexy-smelling segment of the population. We take it pretty seriously.

The process of choosing which love formulas to offer people depends on the variables we can pinpoint in the few minutes we have with a customer that might give a clue as to which form of the God/dess or which particular scent or formula might resonate with them. ("She's a brown lady with copper bangles, maybe Oshun." "This person's a welder, give them Brigid." "They're youthful and poetical, give them Eros.") But this is so very subjective. It takes some trial and error to find what attraction scent works for you.

What about the person who's like, "Hey, I don't do perfumes. Can I still immerse my senses in sexy luxury?" Why, yes! You can! Thanks for asking. You might like to try this super-simple love-drawing bath. All you need is a chai spice tea bag. A lot of the spices that tend to be included in the blend—ginger, cardamom pods, cinnamon, star anise, fennel, peppercorns, nutmeg, or cloves—can be charged and used intentionally to attract love and lust. If you're crazy like me, you might add some powdered milk and a little honey to the bathwater for an extra-sexy body latte.

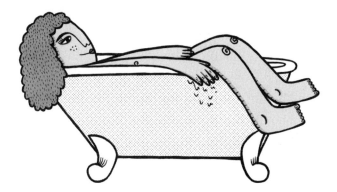

While we're talking about my bathing habits and being embarrassing, let's talk about the love magic I've done and how all of it has worked, but very infrequently the way I meant it to. By that I only mean the pully kind. And of that (I say, blushing and wringing my hands), really just the most innocuous, subtle kind. I may have directed intense focus and intention in a mystical sort of way, but I never consciously did a spell, exactly, to make either or both of the famous, much too old, unavailable, inaccessible, and inadvisable people I fixated my romantic imagination on as a teen, like some perpetual-motion crush-energy reactor, fall in love with me. *But* they did both go on, for whatever reasons, to name their daughters Mya. So they *will* both likely go on to love and cherish Mya for the rest of their lives. The magic worked! But it didn't work. Thankfully so. Everybody's happy now and nobody got magicked into doing something statutory! The universe is really looking out for us all.

Oh, and I found my husband in a pumpkin! But that's a long story.

SUGGESTED READING

Migene González-Wippler, *Santería: The Religion* (Llewellyn, 1989)

Janet and Stewart Farrar, *The Witches' Goddess* (Phoenix Publishing, 1987)

Chapter 10

STACKS AND STACKS OF CASH, OR MONEY DRAWING

I find that money magic is more effective in situations of specific need than general greed. For long-term wealth, it's usually better practice to work on the level of improving your career and drawing customers and acclaim to your business. To attract money to your personal business endeavors, especially for actors, dancers, sex workers, and all stripes of freelancers, prosperity magic can give you a boost, as long as you're doing the work on the earthly plane, too. As above, so below. One of the most important things to remember when you're doing money magic is the very important American ritual of tipping. Abundance magic is about stepping into the flow of riches that exists around you, and you can't do that without getting your feet wet. You have to demonstrate your willingness to participate in the great exchange of capital. You must tip! And if you can, tip more than usual in both amount and frequency while you're working money magic. It doesn't pay to be miserly when you're asking the universe for abundance.

Buy flowers, wear costume jewelry, make yourself into your own ideal imitation of luxury, all while setting some clear goals for what you hope to achieve. With money magic, that means naming a figure. For your first outing, you might not want to set the bar too high. Then envision how this money is going to get to you. Are you going to wait for it to fall from the sky, or are you going to try a new promotional technique for your services? Just like with everything else, you can do spells all day, but if you're not working toward achieving your goals in boring old real life, it's not really gonna work. Doing money magic involves sharpening your eye for opportunity, or at the very least picking up a lottery ticket or something. The dollars you want have to come from somewhere, so you might want to include potential sources of your new wealth when you're visualizing the outcome of your intention.

But in a pinch, Enchantment's money-drawing formula is legend. It smells like cash, and by the magical property of like attracts like, it metaphorically acts like a little money magnet. I can't give out the recipe, but I found this one in *The Magickal Formulary* that I'm happy to share. There must be a thousand recipes by this name:

PROSPERITY POWDER

Allspice

Patchouli

Myrrh

Cinnamon

Sandalwood

Orris

Orange peel

I chose this spell because none of the ingredients are too obscure, and powders are harder to screw up than oils and incense. It doesn't matter if a powder smells crazy because no one has to burn or wear it. It doesn't technically make any difference to the effectiveness of a spell if it smells good or not, but smelling good doesn't hurt.

The operative color in money magic is green, for Venus, the goddess of fertility and lushness. The exchange of currency is a symbolic act, an exchange of promises via little notes. It's almost romantic when you think about it like that. And there again, we have that confluence of love and money; they're always rubbing up against one another, those two. You can use arrowroot powder with a little green food coloring as your base. Allspice, cinnamon, and orange peel are easy grocery store finds. Sandalwood, patchouli, and myrrh are popular perfume oils. The only mystery item is orris, which is just the root of a particular type of iris, so maybe you can dig up something serviceable in the garden if you don't have apothecary access.

Once your ingredients are assembled, grind up some dried orange peel with allspice and cinnamon in a mortar and pestle or coffee grinder and mix it in with the green powder. Then add a few drops of the perfume oils to the mix. Ta-da! We made prosperity powder! What was that? I forgot the orris? I guess I did. I'll put an iris on the altar and consider that base covered. Charge your powder with your vision of an abundant life and put that energy into the mixture as well. The recipe says that you can sprinkle it about the premises or make a circle of it to surround a green candle. You can also sprinkle some in your wallet or on any other tools of your trade. If you prefer to mix the same ingredients up as an oil, incense, bath, or floor wash, go forth and do so!

I just gave you a money-type spell, since I know you wanted it, but I'm not always convinced that money magic is what someone needs, even when money is the most pressing issue. It's often just as likely that what they really needed was an increase in business, a new work opportunity, or a new system for plugging whatever leaks they might have in their piggy bank. When you're doing what you love, when your work is an enactment of you on your path, then money can and will come and rub up against you. Ain't that always the way?

One common source of financial leakage is the habit that so many of us have of undervaluing our skills as it pertains to stacks and stacks of cash. I know I'm not alone in knowing a heap of tremendously talented people who are not receiving compensation commensurate with their expertise. Like chronically. I found an old seal in one of our books at Enchantments for fearlessness in the pursuit of your material goals and I was like, hello! Where have you been all my life? Is that a money spell? Not technically. It's a Martian spell, and we know by now that Mars magic is about fearlessness and active pursuit. I'm finding that the most powerful money magic I've done lately was emptying the very last of my savings in order to buy myself enough time to be a writer. A trust-fall kind of thing. It wasn't a whole lot of money, but it was enough to get me here right now. Trying to make a living at it. I think that's the trick. If you love what you have, you have everything. Maybe only half of abundance magic is the pursuit of treasure. The rest is the process of finding treasure in everything. Even the gift of an empty bank account.

THE CLERK OF SWORDS

We used to sell swords at Enchantments. We had a fairly large selection, some explicitly witchy, others replicas from *Lord of the Rings* and so on. The current owner of the store has disavowed our cosplay roots, but one of my old coworkers from back in the day used to speak fluent Klingon and would trade dollar bills for any Sacagawea gold coins in the cash register so he could store them in a little leather pouch and use them to pay for his mead and turkey legs at the Renaissance festival, which I have to admit is pretty classy.

Anyway, the swords were expensive, so we kept them behind the front counter. I hated selling them. People would ask me elvish questions that I just could not answer, like, "Is this real horn of amaranth on the hilt?" I was done. I was done before we even began. They'd inevitably want to hold, or I guess *wield*, the sword to test its weight and aerodynamics, but I was warned that under no circumstance was I to let them do so, because the cash register had once been robbed by an erstwhile customer cum swashbuckling assailant.

By now we've been through a few examples of devising spells and sigils, so I trust you to go freestyle on this one. Here are some elements you might draw upon while making your own abundance.

CASH MONEY

The colors are green and gold—green for Venus and gold for the sun. The symbols are the kinds of masonic shit you find buried in the whorls of our currency. That pyramid with the eye on top is a trusty seal to carve into a candle, although personally, it always brings to mind the time our ancestors spent toiling for the glory of Pharaoh, which puts me off. Dollar signs, golden coins, and cups that runneth over are also solid choices for focusing your money intentions.

ROAD OPENERS

Gods of the crossroads are many in number but possess strikingly similar qualities and manner. In Hinduism, this spirit is embodied in the form of Ganesha, the elephant-headed god of success, known as the remover of obstacles. Even though he's a big guy, Ganesha is able to get through any tight spots riding on the back of his rodent steed. Ganesha is honored first among the gods and at the outset of any new endeavor, but most specific to his domain are travel, commerce, and writing. He is said to have transcribed the epic tale the Mahabharata with one of his own broken-off tusks. In Santería, Elegua is the keeper of the crossroads. He too is honored first among the orishas and is called upon to banish obstacles in the path of success. He's also associated with commerce and rules over places of coming and going, giving and taking. In the Greek and Roman pantheons Hermes, aka Mercury, bears the role of communicator, the one who watches over the liminal spaces in between things: humanity and the divine, the mundane and the magical. In ancient Egypt this being was known as Thoth, patron of the arts and sciences, magic, and writing. He presides over the greatest spiritual crossroads, as he's the author of the book of the dead. When I think of these gods, my mind also goes to Ananzi, Loki, Br'er Rabbit, Fox and Coyote, Bugs Bunny—all trickster spirits who use their cunning linguistics and preternatural fluidity to make connections and get around the obstacles in the world.

CAREER GOALS

The same way you can use Venusian magic for straight-up cash, or Mars to help you overcome any fear you might have about asserting yourself when it comes to money, and Mercury et alia to help you meet the right people and stay in the loop about fortuitous opportunities, you can ask the favors of the big guy, Jupiter, when it comes to making more out of the business you already have going. Jupiter is all about growth, expansion, and recognition from those in positions of authority. If you're looking to advance a rung up the ladder of your chosen field, Jupiterian magic can give you a leg up. If publicity is what you or your business needs to be successful, you can use solar magic to shine the ultimate spotlight on you and your work. See Chapter 5 for more on all of these planets, and ideas for how to build a ritual to honor their corresponding archetypes.

LUCK

Often luck is the domain of gamblers, so it's sometimes just another kind of money magic, if you ask me. But layering a bit of luck into a spell aimed at attracting something else? Well, now you're cooking. The most prosaic symbols of good luck—the four-leaf clover and lucky horseshoe—are found everywhere in magic. Every candle in glass that we sell at the shop comes with a lucky horseshoe imprinted in the base of the glass. I've seen it there so often I don't notice it anymore, but its effect is that every spell we do is a petition for good fortune of some variety. Another symbol folks use toward these talismanic ends is the hamsa, or hand of Fatima, a Middle Eastern and North African symbol meant to represent the hand of God, warding off evil and attracting luck and blessings.

WISHES

Maybe you prefer to make your own luck. You might like to try wishing magic, if you have something very specific in mind. Here are a few luck and wishing items that may not be quite so familiar to you. They're not the easiest items to find in stores, but not quite as difficult to locate as a four-leaf clover.

- Rose of Jericho. The rose of Jericho is not in fact a rose, but a dried-up, gnarled, clawlike little tumbleweed. With just a bit of moisture, the gnarled claw revives into a living plant and unfurls into a lotus blossom shape. For this, it's also known as the resurrection plant and was used by Christian missionaries to illustrate the concept of spiritual rebirth. Hoodoo and folk magic practitioners use the water from the rose of Jericho to lure prosperity into the home. For wishing magic, write your wish on a slip of paper and put it in the center of the open "rose." When you remove it from the water the plant will close around it, enveloping your wish.

- Job's tears. Not to be confused with Job's actual biblical tears, Job's tears is an extra-large variety of millet, a smooth beadlike seed said to bring good luck if you carry three of them at a time. But if you carry seven such seeds for seven days while focusing on a wish, your wish will come true when you release the seeds in running water.
- Tonka beans. Tonka is prized for its vanilla-like scent and delicate smoky flavor, although it's considered toxic by the FDA. So I guess don't eat it? Or just don't tell anyone that I told you to eat it. But feel free to make use of this Central American legume in love- and luck-drawing mixtures, or simply visualize your wish while holding a bean and then release it to running water, the preferred means of magical conveyance.

Chapter 11

THE MANCY LIST, OR DIVINATION

Divination is a means of gaining some insight or new perspective on a given situation from the intuitive deciphering of cards, images, thrown bones or stones, or any other symbolically charged item. There are so many forms of divination it boggles the mind. You could probably figure out a way to divine with Boggle if you really wanted to. Any mystical attempt to find an answer to a question, be it via crystal ball or a Magic 8-Ball, is a form of divination. Which tools or materials you decide to use to clarify a confusing situation or find a useful strategy for moving forward from a tough spot are not super-important. What *is* critical is that whatever method you use feels like a language that you want to learn. Divination is a translation process, a method of identifying patterns within a seemingly chaotic system. Like that movie where Jodie Foster listens to the detuned radio static of outer space through satellite dishes in the desert until she manages to locate the message encoded in the fuzzy noise. It seems to me that most systems of divination require a certain amount of fuzzy noise or randomness that, when filtered through a closed system of logic, begins to coalesce into the shape of a story . . . about you and all your problems. For dear Jodie Foster in *Contact*, she filters the random noise of the universe into a closed system of binary code, 1's and 0's that reveal a hidden message from aliens.

In divination, the source of the information is, if possible, even hazier and harder to prove than aliens, and I tend to zone out when people try to explain exactly where the information gleaned actually comes from. I don't care very much, because once you're convinced that a method or practitioner works, the results are so uncanny and the experience so rewarding that the "why" questions tend to go out the window. Maybe it's spirits, or angels, or fairies invisibly stacking the deck of cards in just the right order. None of it makes much of a difference in the face of the refreshing perspective that a skilled diviner can offer.

That said, I'd like to present some tips and best practices for people who get divinatory readings:

- It's a good idea to have some positive reference for the reader, a recommendation from a friend or institution you trust. I'm not a big proponent of fortune-tellers who pull people in off the street.
- Be wary of people who have a constantly escalating price point or construct their advice in such a way as to necessitate your coming back to them for readings over and over again. Getting readings every so often is one thing, but if a reader seems to be

manipulating you into a dependent relationship instead of inspiring you to trust your intuition, take your own counsel, and control your own life, then, knowingly or not, they're not doing you any great service. My friend who reads cards at Enchantments told me that he always likes to have people leave a reading with either good news or a plan of action to address whatever distressing situations were brought to the surface during the reading process. That's the kind of reader you're gonna want to look for.

- Come in with an open mind. Let the process happen. Bring a pen and paper to record the reading. Some folks will let you use your phone to record, or take a picture of the cards. Don't be afraid to ask questions and follow up where appropriate. The reading is supposed to be a tool, so your reader should be available to help you learn how to use it.

- But do also come in with a few questions or areas of life to guide your reading toward. Most readings will offer a general overview of things; it's up to you to focus your reader's attention.

- Choose a meditation card during tarot readings. If there's one card that particularly draws your attention during your reading, make a special note of it and spend some time researching its associations and symbolic meanings. Tarot is learned one card at a time. It's easier to remember the meanings of the cards when applied to an emotionally charged situation.

If tarot's not your thing, there are countless forms of divination to investigate and practice yourself, each of them a complex, detailed system that I can hardly do justice to here. The following will give you a taste of some of the major types, to help you determine which you might want to learn more about, followed by a bonkers list of some arcane forms of divination that may remain arcane for a reason.

THE RUNES

The runes are an ancient Norse symbolic alphabet that are inscribed on stones or hard wood; you *cast*, or kinda toss, them onto a surface, and read the results according to ascribed meanings for each rune, their positions (upright or reversed), and their relationships to each other (distant or touching, etc.). There are specific ways of casting the runes for different sorts of questions or explanations. For example, you can pull three at random while considering your situation, and read them as past, present, and future. The system is connected to the Norse concept of *wyrd* or fate. Not fate as in "inescapable and preordained," but fate as in "how the future will be if you continue your present course of action." In the runes, as in all forms of divination, there is always room for free will. If that wasn't the case, what good would divination do? Everything would already be settled and there wouldn't be a reason to do anything about anything. But within the closed system of the runes (or the tarot, or the I Ching, or Boggle for that matter), all the possibilities of the universe are available to be expressed and interpreted. Different avenues of action can be considered and tested.

PENDULUMS

A pendulum is any weight on a chain or string, but some folks like to get fancy and use semiprecious stones. Nette gave me an amethyst one that someone else gave her. The pendulum, like all forms of divination, is a way to access and interpret your own voice of inner knowingness. Pendulum work is directional—gravity makes the weighted end move while you hold the other end up and try to keep your hand still, and different directions are indicated by its swaying. It's based on the principle that if you applied the pointing power of the pendulum to some sort of closed system, like a map, or even a sheet of paper with different options indicated in different areas, the pendulum would indicate the answer to a question. Because of that, they're often used to help locate people, places, or things. But most of all, pendulums are excellent meditative aids. Closely observing their seemingly random movements has a similar effect to watching the flickering of a candle flame. It is just stimulating enough to release the rest of your mind from its chatter and allow for a wordless sort of abstraction. That semi-trance abstraction is the frame of mind that best serves divination. Sometimes I don't have a pendulum on me. Okay, almost all the time I don't have a pendulum on me, but luckily I've found that I have a pendulum *in me*! And you do, too. I'll explain. I have this very luxurious problem called "a car in Brooklyn." It's not very smart to have a car in Brooklyn, but I have my reasons and my excuses and my little witchy methods of dealing with the perennial problem of alternate-side parking. I get in my car, and before I start circling the block forever, I close my eyes and try to reach that cool abstracted pendulum state of mind while visualizing the grid of streets around my house; in my mind's eye, it looks a bit like the layout of a Pac-Man game. If I can relax and make myself still, I find my own inner pendulum will nudge me toward a certain part of the mental map where one of those little dots on the arcade board lights up to indicate a potential parking spot, and I try to make it over there before some other Pac-Man gobbles it up. I haven't exactly made a science of it (LOL, this isn't science), but it's worked a bunch of times, so much so that I've decided to tape a real-life map of my neighborhood to my dashboard to see if my success rate goes up.

DOWSING RODS

A dowsing rod can be a Y-shaped stick or two L-shaped sticks or metal rods that are used to locate anything of interest beneath the earth, usually underground sources of water. Not much call for these in Brooklyn. The water's in the pipes, blessedly. (So far. I'd hate to speak too soon.) The dowser holds the stick or sticks and surveys the land sort of like one would do with a metal detector. But while a metal detector works by emitting a magnetic field that responds with a beep when it encounters metal, the dowsing rods work by responding to your vibes, or the vibes of what you're looking for. When you've located the spring, the buried pipe, or the gold doubloons that you seek, the end of the Y will point it out to you, or the L-shaped rods will form themselves into an X to mark the spot. The practice has its roots in Renaissance-era magic and is notably used today by water utilities in the United Kingdom, although it hasn't been proven to work any better than just guessing where the water might be.

FAQ: MUMBLE, MUMBLE, MUMBLE, SOMETHING ABOUT A OUIJA BOARD

More often than one might imagine, people call up Enchantments, stuttering, mumbling, and asking something about Ouija boards: how to use them, what they're used for, and if it's demons. The last time this happened I told the person on the other end that a Ouija board is a toy, so they should probably try using it to have fun with their friends, but they didn't like that answer. They said, "But no, really . . . ," as if they thought I was just holding out to see if they could handle the *real truth* about Ouija. The truth is that although there have been "talking boards" throughout history, the Ouija was patented and mass-produced as a parlor game, and popularized by spiritualists as a way to communicate with the dead. The original patent holder sold out to Parker Brothers in the 1960s, and the board hasn't changed much since you were at a sleepover in the seventh grade. The name *Ouija* is, incidentally, just a combination of the French and German words for "yes."

PALMISTRY

True confession: I was a fake-ass palm reader! I only did it once, okay? And I don't think I was really swindling anybody because it was free and I was wearing a silly costume. It was clearly *for novelty purposes only.* I'm lucky it was before our phones had cameras worth a damn, or we'd have to: [insert photo]. It was a Harry Potter release party at McNally Jackson, a bookstore in Soho. Fancy! $$! I had a job! (+1), but I had little to no knowledge of palmistry (-1). I had a lot of chutzpah (+1) and a cape (+1), and access to the witchcraft store (+ a zillion). I figured I could pull it off. I went to Enchantments and found the one book with anything about palmistry in it, then took some fevered notes on a legal pad to memorize on the train ride there. I think I even cribbed a few things on my own palm so I wouldn't confuse anyone's head and heart lines. It could have been a mess, but my Enchantments skills kicked in and I cold-read those book enthusiasts like a pro . . . or maybe a con. As it turns out, holding a stranger's hand and sharing your undivided attention with them for a few minutes is pretty powerful magic on its own. All of my marks left happy.

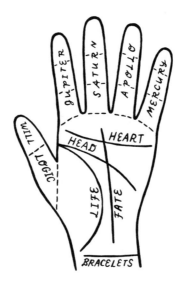

I still don't know much about palmistry, but in a nutshell, the process involves attaching significance to the characteristics of the hand, fingers, and the lines of the palm in order to read a person's fate or destiny. The general shape and quality of the hand is often thought of in terms of the elements—an earth hand is square, rough, and fat-fingered, a water hand is more elongated in the palm with tapered fingers, the fire hand has a long palm and relatively short fingers, and the air hand is square-palmed and long-fingered. The different shapes reflect the general temperament of the questioner. The character of the lines and mounts, or fleshy pads, on the palm reflect the nature of the questioner's destiny. But the destiny-reading model is difficult for me to appreciate. As far as I can see, it can only tell you (a) things you already know about yourself—for instance, that you are creative or practical—and (b) things that you can't do anything but worry about, like having a short life line, or a faint and broken heart line. That said, I know there must be truly gifted palm readers out there, and I mean them no offense by my ignorance of their art.

THE TAROT

I don't personally practice any one form of divination with regularity, but I *am* in a perpetual state of "trying to learn the tarot," like so many people who make it most of the way through the section on the Major Arcana in a tarot book and then quietly move on to something else. The tarot is complicated! It's a whole new symbolic language, although—wait, I shouldn't say that, because it's anything but new, it's just new to me and you. The tarot has many origin myths owing to the fact that it contains the symbology of many different mystic systems: astrology, Gnosticism, alchemy, ritual magic, and Kabbalah, to name a few. When I try to read tarot, I usually have the little booklet that comes with the cards in one hand, which is like trying to have a deep conversation via Google Translate. You get the gist, but you miss all the nuance. But practice makes competence, right? Just like learning any language, you have to put the time in to gain the fluency you need to read with confidence.

Dilettante though I am, I can still tell you a few things about tarot as a system, starting with the definition of the phrase "Major Arcana," which I glossed over a second ago like you should already know what it means. Most tarot decks consist of two component sets of cards, the Major Arcana and the Minor Arcana. There's endless variation between decks in terms of the imagery used to convey each card's significance. Some of the oldest tarot cards, like the Visconti Sforza collection and the Tarot of Marseilles, date back to the fifteenth century. A more recent iteration, dating from 1910, is the Rider-Waite deck, and it is still widely considered the standard, which is to say that most tarot books reference its symbology. The Major Arcana is a collection of twenty-two cards that depict archetypal figures and universal concepts. In most decks the Major Arcana consist of the following: *the Fool, the Magician, the High Priestess, the Empress, the Emperor, the Hierophant, the Lovers, the Chariot, Strength, the Hermit, Wheel of Fortune, Justice, the Hanged Man, Death, Temperance, the Devil, the Tower, the Star, the Moon, the Sun, Judgement,* and *the World.* The Minor Arcana are fifty-six suit cards that correspond to a regular deck of playing cards: four suits with fourteen cards each that are comparable to the one to ten number cards and four face cards. But where the Marseilles deck is illustrated with playing-card motifs, most tarot decks have evolved to include heavily symbolic scenes on the Minor Arcana, too. These cards are used to elucidate the finer points of the questioner's situation, while the Major Arcana deal with, you guessed it, major stuff.

Jung famously deemed the Major Arcana of the tarot *archetypes*, means of accessing the wisdom of the collective unconscious, not intended so much to tell the future in a prognosticating way as to elucidate the present in light of the past. By the collective unconscious, Jung is talking about an even more misty, mystical antiquity than usual; he's talking about the basic operating system of the human being, the non-cognitive function of the brain that tells us to seek shelter when exposed, fear predators, hunt prey, and seek sex and companionship. There's nothing new under the Sun card, you know what I mean? Whatever you call it, that complement of urges and ways of being is hardwired into all of us, and the tarot just happens to have developed into a complete system we can subconsciously direct to tell us a story about our lives. It's like a wise old crone who you think must be psychic but really she's not telling the future, she's just extrapolating from her deep knowledge of the past. In the case of tarot, it's deep knowledge of the past of *all humankind*, the base programming that apparently only needs seventy-eight cards as variables in order to be able to tell the story of everyone's life. It would seem improbable until you remember that it only takes twenty-three pairs of chromosomes to program the full biodiversity of the human race, twenty-six letters that make up the English language. So maybe it's not so strange that a deck of seventy-eight evocative images makes up a language that we can use to communicate with our own inner knowing. In fact, that's the false wall I tend to run into when I think about divination, and tarot specifically—I find that a tarot reading, even one from a very attuned and inspired reader, will only tell me things that I already know. And then I find myself yelling at a deck of cards, like, *"Yeah,* so what? What am I supposed to *do?"*

Ultimately, the cards can't give you all the answers about the future, but they do offer a great opportunity to meditate on

the present in light of the past, and to look forward from there. It can be immensely helpful to have inklings and suspicions confirmed by the cards, or to have unnecessary worry laid to rest by their insistence that your fears are imagined. Even when I'm reading for myself, piecemeal, one card at a time, looking up the meanings every five seconds and waffling and stressing over which interpretation to take, I usually get some new slant of insight out of the experience.

But if you find that all of the abovementioned methods of divination are too trendy and newfangled for your tastes, here follows the arcane and amusing Mancy List, borrowed and adapted from Paranormal-Encyclopedia.com. I include it here firstly because these are some of my shiniest new favorite words, and I want to show them off to you, but also because they serve to further illustrate the point that when it comes to divination the most important tool is the one you dig the most. Also, I love to think of J. K. Rowling poring over this kind of list when devising her Hogwarts syllabi. Love you, J. K.! Shouts to Snape!

MANCY CHART

Natural elements or conditions

AIR AND ATMOSPHERE (AEROMANCY)

Wind: austomancy
Thunder and lightning: ceraunoscopy/keraunomancy
Aerial visions: chaomancy
Sound of thunder: bronoscopy
Meteors, shooting stars: meteromancy
Moon phase and appearance: selenomancy

WATER

Observing ripples, ebb and flow: hydromancy/ydromancy
Finding water: water witching

FIRE

Fire: pyromancy

STONES

Crystals or semiprecious stones: lithomancy

PLANTS

Petals—sound produced by slapping against hand: phyllorho-domancy

ANIMALS (ZOOMANCY)

Cats: ailuromancy
Horses: hippomancy
Rodents: myomancy
Serpents: ophiomancy
Birds: ornithomancy

INSECTS (ENTOMANCY)

Spiders: arachnomancy
Ants: myrmomancy
Beetle tracks: skatharomancy

Man-made objects

TOOLS

Arrows: belomancy/bolomancy
Cards: cartomancy
Computers: cybermancy
Spinning tops, bottles, or wheels: cyclomancy
Pendulums: pallomancy
Suspended rings: dactyliomancy/dactlomancy
Rods or sticks: rhabdomancy
Rods to find water: water witching

WRITING

Paper messages in pastry: aleuromancy
Random passages from books: bibliomancy
Handwriting: graphology

BOOKS (BIBLIOMANCY)

Books by Homer or Virgil: stoichemancy
Books of poetry: rhapsodomancy

FOOD AND DRINK

Wine: oenomancy/olinomancy
Cheese: tiromancy/typomancy/tyromancy
Tea leaves, coffee grounds, wine sediments: tasseography/
tasseomancy

Numbers

NUMBER SYSTEMS (ARITHMANCY)

Hebrew numerology: gematria
Dates and words converted to numbers: numerology
Position of stars at birth: genethialogy/natal astrology

Human body

ANATOMY

Hand, palm, finger(nail)s: cheiromancy/chiromancy
Caul at birth: amniomancy
Eye: oculomancy
Foot: podomancy

WASTE

Feces: scatamancy
Urine: uromancy/urimancy

RITUAL SACRIFICE

Human sacrifice: anthropomancy/antipomancy/splanchamancy
Animal sacrifice: hiromancy/hieroscopy

HUMAN ACTIVITY OR REACTION

Walking dizzily around a circle marked with letters: gyromancy
Laughter: geloscopy
Dreams: oneiromancy
Communion with the dead: necromancy
Accidental seeing or hearing: transataumancy
Location of itch: urticariomancy
Encounters with strangers: xenomancy
Gazing into objects: scrying

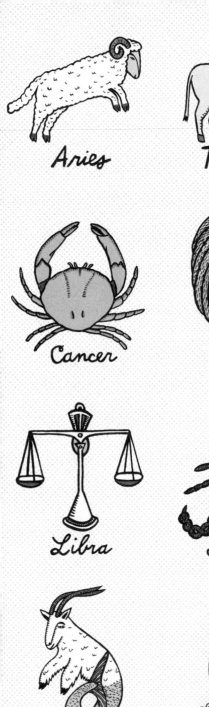

Aries

Taurus

Gemini

Cancer

Leo

Virgo

Libra

Scorpio

Sagittarius

Capricorn

Aquarius

Pisces

Chapter 12

THE WHOLE FUCKING SOLAR SYSTEM, OR ASTROLOGY

Witches—and, come to think of it, lots of people who wouldn't identify as such—use the systems that make up the study of astrology in the interest of understanding ourselves and other people. As a form of divination, birth chart astrology is meant to shed light on the different ways that the configurations of the planets and stars at the moment of a person's birth can influence how an individual approaches life, relationships with others, and relationship with oneself. In addition to helping you interpret your birth chart, a skilled astrologer will take into consideration the transits, or movements, of the planets as they pertain to your particular chart. If nothing else, studying the basic tenets of astrology reminds me that there's no one way to live a good life. There are at least twelve ways! Maybe more, but you'll have to convince me.

To start, you gotta know the twelve signs of the zodiac, and they're not exactly the twelve lost tribes of Atlantis, so this part is easy. We've already discussed the magical influences of the planets and luminaries (see Chapter 5), so we're ahead of the game when it comes to learning the characters of the signs. Each sign is particularly influenced, or ruled, by a certain planetary energy. Some planets rule over two signs, and some signs have two rulers, but don't worry about keeping all this info in your head. That's what charts are for.

You'll find one here with the signs and their corresponding symbols, plus the adorable catchphrases that give you an idea of what each sign's collective perspective or energy is all about. These zodiacal associations will be important toward the end of this chapter, when we try to make sense of your own birth chart.

Before I forget to mention it, the signs of the zodiac are constellations! That is to say, they're groupings of stars in which we humans see meaningful images, twelve meaningful images that the planets and luminaries seem to travel through from our vantage point here on earth. A person's sun sign or zodiac sign is determined by where the sun was at the time of their birth. The sun moves from one constellation to the next every month, give or take a few days. I list the dates for each sign beginning and ending on the twenty-first of the month, but that's just an approximation.

THE SIGNS OF THE ZODIAC

Aries: March 21–April 21

That's supposed to look like the head of the ram, coming at you horns first. The symbol is also meant to remind you of the human head and brow, the body parts associated with Aries, the first sign of the zodiac. The Aries attitude is often summed up in the phrase "I am." If you think about the progression of the signs in terms of the development of a person, Aries is that brand-new baby stage. Once you pop out of the womb, your immediate instincts are what matter most. Aries are known to be impulsive because they're living in the moment. They're ruled by the planet Mars, as characterized by the aggressive, assertive Roman god of war. Aries is fiery, active, and spontaneous. They're always trying to get things done. If you need to ask an Aries for a favor, present it as a challenge, a *Mission: Impossible* scenario that needs to be accomplished right now! Appeal to their sense of adventure.

Taurus: April 21–May 21

That's the sign of the bull. It doesn't seem to be charging at you like Aries, but it doesn't look likely to move out of anyone's way anytime soon. The shape of the symbol is meant to resemble the chin, mouth, and throat region. The Taurus motto is "I have," and they're ruled by the planet Venus, the goddess of love and beauty. They're earthly people, enamored of patterns and textures, especially the tactile stuff: "What can I have that's beautiful? Can I have delicious food? Can I have delicious linens? Can I have a delicious nap?" Taureans (Tauri? Tauruses?) are known for being particularly stubborn. They're associated with the toddler stage of life. They know who they are and what they want, but they are not particularly celebrated for their communication skills. They just refuse, passive-resistance style. Taurus is an earth sign, as we'll discuss later, so they tend to pay attention to their money and possessions. Taureans (and toddlers) are big on security. Need a favor from a Taurus? Feed them first. Ask them while they've got something delicious in their mouth. Bear gifts.

Gemini: May 21–June 21

Those two connected lines are the famous twins from Greek and Roman mythology, Castor and Pollux. Gemini rules the arms, hands, shoulders, and lungs, all of those twin organs. Their attitude is summed up in the credo "I think." They're concerned primarily with ideas and communication. The sign is associated with the developmental stage where the child begins to express their ideas and understand other people's responses. Perhaps because of the twinlike duality of the sign, Gemini energy is considered both active and receptive (+/-, masculine/feminine . . . more on this later) but it gets classified as active when it has to choose. It's ruled by Mercury, the androgynous messenger god of communication and exchange. If you have to ask a Gemini for a favor, come right out with the terms of the bargain. You should offer to barter or make it worth their while in terms of the connections they might gain in the process. It's a two-way street with a Gemini. Two is kinda their thing.

Cancer: June 21–July 21

It's a crab! At least the Greeks called it a crab. The Egyptians and Babylonians thought of it as more of a tortoise. Everyone agrees that it's a creature who wears its home on its back. Cancer is about home, in all senses of the word: the way you relate to your childhood, the sort of home you want to make for yourself in the present, and, ultimately, what home means to you emotionally. It corresponds with the preschool-age kid who's just starting to have a life outside of the home and thus developing that necessary, portable sense of security. Their motto is "I feel," and like all water signs (I know, I know, I'll explain soon), they are particularly concerned with emotions. The symbol is meant to remind you of some boobs, or breasts if you're mature—the protective padding over the heart, the part of the body associated with Cancer. Cancer is not ruled by a planet; it's ruled by the moon. The moon moves through the signs very quickly, so some say that's why Cancers are known for being a bit moody. How to ask a Cancer for a favor? Make it seem like an emergency. Let them know how much you hate to ask. Go over the top, and send a thank-you note while you're at it.

Leo: July 21–August 21

That shape right there is supposed to look like a lion. It . . . doesn't. The glyph is also meant to remind you of the valves of the human heart, the body part attributed to Leo. "I will" is their motto, and as a fire sign (we'll talk more about this later, really soon, I'm sorry), they're inclined toward action and doing. Unlike the other fire sign we mentioned, Aries, they don't run at what they want headfirst; lions prefer to stalk their prey. They're strategic. They take their time. Leo is ruled by the sun, the center of our solar system. They're warm, bright, and animated, and they want your attention. If you want a favor from them, you should probably kiss their ass. Seriously, tell them how wonderful they are. You'd think they would be too good for that kind of thing, since a Leo knows their own worth, but they still wanna hear it.

Virgo: August 21–September 21

The virgin in question is Astraea, goddess of innocence and purity, the last of the immortals to abandon the earth after Pandora opened that box full of chaos; Astraea is honored by the gods for her fortitude. Let the glyph's twists and turns remind you of your digestive tract and intestines. Now that you're hungry, I'll remind you that the timing of the sun's passage through the Virgo constellation corresponds to the harvest season, and Virgo's most prominent star is Spica, whose name means "ear of corn" or "sheaf of wheat." All of this leads me to think of Virgos as farmers, industrious, practical, and grounded. Their words are "I analyze," and like the high school stage of life that they're associated with, they're focused on learning about how things work and fit together: systems analysis, tinkering. Virgos are ruled by Mercury, so they're interested in making connections, but since Virgo is the sign of service, they make connections through their good deeds and labor. How to get a favor from a Virgo: be polite, and make it very easy for them. They sincerely want to do you a favor if they can.

Libra: September 21–October 21

Those are the scales that Anubis, the Egyptian jackal-headed god, or Themis, the Greek embodiment of justice, uses to weigh the souls of the dead against the feather of truth. You can interpret the glyph as the sacrum, the flat lower back area, the back of the hips, and the buttocks. Their words are "I balance," and combined with the influence of their ruling planet, Venus (intimacy and love), they seek balance and harmony between people. In our developmental stage corollary, Libra corresponds to the late teens, when some people start dating or wanting to; they tend to feel stronger as a part of a team. Libras want to make things with other people and have pleasing intellectual conversations with other people. They want to appreciate books, music, and art with other people. Libra is more than happy to do you a favor; their reward is the opportunity for intimacy and connection that doing the favor will bring.

Scorpio: October 21–November 21

That's the pointy tail of the scorpion. Legend has it that this is the very same scorpion that killed Orion the hunter in a dramatic turn played out in the sky when the seasons shift and the hunter's constellation fades into the horizon as the scorpion rises. Badass. All deep and sensual, Scorpio rules the genitals and reproductive organs, so desire and creation are the themes. Scorpio's words are "I create," just in case you weren't sure. In terms of developmental stages, I'll go ahead and call this a ho phase. They're trying on their adult selves, having the sex, the heartbreak, the getting over it. Scorpio is an emotionally driven sign ruled by Mars, so Scorpios are known for the smoldering depth of their passion. Want a favor from a Scorpio? If you're in their inner circle, you'll barely need to ask. They'll probably offer. But if you know they don't fuck with you like that, you shouldn't bother.

Sagittarius: November 21–December 21

The glyph is the arrow of the centaur, half person and half horse, specifically Chiron, a supremely learned, skilled, and exalted character in Greek mythology. He wasn't just a centaur, he was a mentor! It's a teacherly sign associated with higher learning, athletic teams, frats, and other forms of hierarchy and merit. It's the college years! The key words are "I perceive," so they're sharp-eyed and calculating, able to still themselves, like an archer, before taking their shot. Sadge is ruled by Jupiter, which is all about growth and expansion. Want a favor from a Sadge? Make it festive! Buy them a drink. They are the most generous and optimistic in the zodiac. But beware of excess: Sadge rules the liver (hips and thighs, too). Make it sound like fun, and they're down for whatever.

Capricorn: December 21–January 21

The glyph is a sea goat. Enough said. That should be obvious. Everyone knows what a sea goat is. For real, though, it's a goat on top and a fish on the bottom, in the form of the Babylonian god Ea, the ruler of the underground sea that was thought to cause the Tigris and Euphrates Rivers to flood annually. Capricorn's motto is "I use." When you come out of grad school with, like, your MBA or whatever, and put your skills to work, that's the Capricorn phase of life. Capricorns are oriented toward being professional grown-ups. They're ambitious, and they take *the rules* very seriously. They have a plan of attack: they know how to find the resources they need, and they know how to use them. Patience and caution are their key words. Capricorn is ruled by Saturn, which you may remember as the opposite of Jupiter. Jupiter's all about pushing limits, while Saturn is about keeping within them. Saturn is discipline, restriction. That's why Saturn and Jupiter are used together in magic that concerns futzing around with the legal system. Interesting, huh? Capricorn rules the bones and teeth. They're structured. If you need to ask something of a Capricorn, do so well in advance. If it fits their schedule, you're golden. They won't do much on the spur of the moment, but they'll pencil anything in for family.

Aquarius: January 21–February 21

The water-bearer constellation started as a reference to the Egyptian god Hapi, the embodiment of the life-giving waters of the Nile, but later was attributed to Ganymede, sommelier to the gods. Aquarius's motto is "I know," and it's correlated with the period of life where one is no longer seeking the approval of any authority but oneself. Aquarius has tenure, Aquarius has its pension. Independence is an Aquarian theme. Aquarius is ruled by Saturn, like Capricorn. But where Capricorns stick to the rules and get their shit done, Aquarians take the ethic of discipline and restriction and apply it to ideas rather than working systems. Aquarius rules everything between the feet and the knees; the shins, the calves, the ankles. Aquarius uses ideas and information to connect with others. How do you get a favor from an Aquarius? Do your best to understand their limits. Be willing to accept a no. They'll come through for you in their own way.

Pisces: February 21–March 21

This shape is meant to inspire visions of two fish, tied together by their tails. The associated fishes of myth are considered by some to be representations of the Tigris and Euphrates Rivers and by others to be Venus and her son Cupid, disguised as fish to escape a monster. You can also think of the two lines as the two feet, as Pisces rules that part of the body. "I believe" is their motto, and it corresponds to old age, ideally a mellow, reflective time. Pisces are very fluid. They're slippery. Pisces is the end of the cycle, but that means that it's poised to slip past mortal boundaries. It's the sign of the great monks and spiritualists. Pisces is ruled by Jupiter and Neptune. Jupiter is vast, like the expanse of the ocean, but it's a water sign, so it's an emotional ocean. As for Neptune, it is the realm of inspirations and fantasies. Sometimes, illusion. When you go down to the bottom of the ocean, things aren't what they seem. How do you get a Pisces to do a favor? Appeal to their sense of whimsy.

COMPARE AND CONTRAST

Now that we know a bit about each sign we can start thinking of them in terms of their group associations, and how the different groupings can be understood collectively. One way to break down the group of twelve signs is by their element.

> **Earth** is Virgo, Capricorn, Taurus.
> **Air** is Gemini, Libra, Aquarius.
> **Fire** is Aries, Leo, Sagittarius.
> **Water** is Cancer, Scorpio, Pisces.

The **earth** signs are known collectively for their industriousness, and particularly their mastery over the basic stuffs of life: diligence and maintenance. Earth signs are good with practice, business, and physical labor. Earth signs are good at maps. Earth signs can feed the whole gang of people who showed up at your house uninvited, loaves and fishes style, even though there wasn't anything in the fridge but mustard and baking soda. I'm talking about you, Taurus, Virgo, and Capricorn.

The **air** signs are all about communication and logic, which follows when you think about the way that air carries ideas via our breath, enabling the intangible power of ideas to move from person to person invisibly. Air signs delight in communication, in making connection and making sense of things. The air signs are Gemini, Libra, and Aquarius.

Fire signs are action-oriented. They learn through doing, they're kinetic, enthusiastic, spontaneous, and not averse to conflict and or attention. They're known for spontaneity and their ability to transform. A generative spark. They're all about the present moment. Aries, Leo, and Sagittarius are our fire signs.

Water signs tend to see things through a personal, emotional, and creative lens. Their actions are often driven by the pursuit of emotional satisfaction. Like water, they're known to be deep, reflective, and sensitive to the vibrations around them. Water signs are Cancer, Scorpio, and Pisces.

POLARITIES

I don't want to perpetuate a bunch of weird gendered crap with the way I characterize these polarities, so I've landed on "projecting" and "receptive" as my signifiers, but know that you'll find them described in several ways: masculine and feminine, positive and negative, active and passive. I think of it this way: Where Aries (+) is focused on wanting what it wants, Taurus (-) is focused on keeping what it has. Where Gemini (+) seeks connection actively, Cancer (-) locks that connection down at home. Where Leo (+) seeks glamor and attention, Virgo (-) seeks simplicity and order. Where Libra (+) will bend over backward to maintain a sense of balance, Scorpio (-) doesn't mind friction and takes imbalance as a matter of course. Where Sagittarius (+) is expansive and gregarious, Capricorn (-) is rule-oriented and industrious. Where Aquarius (+) engages, Pisces (-) eludes. This reciprocal system of balanced energies is at the root of a lot of magical logic, and, not coincidentally, a lot of real spooky advanced physics.

MODALITIES

Modalities are the modus operandi of a sign. They're broken down into three groups:

> **Cardinal** is Aries, Cancer, Libra, Capricorn.
> **Fixed** is Aquarius, Leo, Scorpio, Taurus.
> **Mutable** is Gemini, Virgo, Sagittarius, Pisces.

Their meanings aren't obvious, so let's go a little deeper into each one.

Cardinal signs initiate each season: Aries for spring, Cancer in summer, Libra in autumn, and Capricorn for winter. They're born leaders, champions, and instigators. Generally, cardinal signs are the influencers who push the other signs toward some goal. Cardinal signs have an agenda and an itinerary.

Fixed signs are set in their ways. They remain steady even when others try to influence them, for better or worse. They don't really adjust to other people; other people adjust to them. If you're making plans with a fixed person, be sure to hold up your end of the bargain. You've got to fit into the space they've carved out for you.

Mutable means changeable, adaptable. Mutable signs adjust to other people and their environment. You know you're making plans with a mutable person because they dunno, they're free, they're around. Whenever you can do it is fine with them, really! Flexibility is the watchword.

SIGN	SYMBOL	DATES	PLANET(S)
ARIES	♈	3/21–4/21	♂ Mars
TAURUS	♉	4/21–5/21	♀ Venus
GEMINI	♊	5/21–6/21	☿ Mercury
CANCER	♋	6/21–7/21	☽ Moon
LEO	♌	7/21–8/21	☉ Sun
VIRGO	♍	8/21–9/21	☿ Mercury
LIBRA	♎	9/21–10/21	♀ Venus
SCORPIO	♏	10/21–11/21	♂ Mars/Pluto
SAGITTARIUS	♐	11/21–12/21	♃ Jupiter
CAPRICORN	♑	12/21–1/21	♄ Saturn
AQUARIUS	♒	1/21–2/21	♄/♅ Saturn/ Uranus
PISCES	♓	2/21–3/21	♃/♆ Jupiter/ Neptune

POLARITY, MODALITY	ELEMENT	KEY WORDS	BODY PART
Projecting, cardinal	Fire	I am	head/brow
Receptive, fixed	Earth	I have	mouth/throat
Neutral, mutable	Air	I think	arms, lungs
Receptive, cardinal	Water	I feel	chest/breasts
Projecting, fixed	Fire	I will	solar plexus
Receptive, mutable	Earth	I analyze	digestive system
Projecting, cardinal	Air	I balance	lower back/hips
Receptive, fixed	Water	I create	sex organs
Projecting, mutable	Fire	I see	liver/haunches
Receptive, cardinal	Earth	I use	bones, teeth, spine
Projecting, fixed	Air	I know	shins/ankles
Receptive, mutable	Water	I believe	feet

Now that we have the signs and the planets all sorted out, we're ready to take a look at our birth charts! Goody for us.

BIRTH CHARTS

A birth chart is a snapshot of the sky when and where an individual was born. When you layer the wheel of the zodiac over that round sky map of the birth moment, you can use it like a magnifying lens to study the different aspects and patterns that arise in the person in question. For beginners like us, the most useful things to know about your birth chart are your sun, moon, and rising signs. You probably know what your *sun sign* is by now (the sign that the sun was passing through when you were born), but if you're not sure, take a look at pages 194–195 and check the chart for your birthday. Your sun sign is meant to indicate the overall flavor of your vibe and what motivates you. For example, I am a Pisces (February 21– March 21, "I believe"), and here you find me writing a book about spirituality and mysticism. True to Piscean form, I'm sensitive and emotional, and at times I've been known to be emotionally sensitive. I'm dreamy and weird and I could spend all my waking hours in the bath if someone would just feed me periodically and make sure I haven't fallen asleep in there. It happens. Not every Pisces is going to believe or behave in the same way, or do the same sort of work with their Piscean proclivities, but the theories behind astrology persist because they really do add up in the end.

Your *rising sign* is the constellation that was rising on the eastern horizon at the time of your birth. It's the energy of the outward projection of your personality. For example, my rising sign is Leo, and unlike my misty water-colored sun sign,

Leo rising people tend to project an outgoing, performative, and confident vibe. They give the impression that they might prefer to spend an evening in front of an audience more than, say, eating in their bathtub like some fishy Pisces. Catlike, they crave admiration, but only the right kind and at the right time. Their standards are high. Leo is a bright, warm, attractive sign, like the sun, which rules Leo.

Your *moon sign* is the constellation the moon was in at the time of your birth. It's indicative of the character of your relationship to yourself, the kind of energy you direct inward. So deep! I'm still working out my understanding of my moon sign. I feel super-conflicted about it. Sometimes I'm like, yeah, Gemini! It's ruled by Mercury, and Mercury rules the areas of life that fascinate me: communication, ideas, the connections between people, the poetry, the magic, the spark of genius. And then sometimes, I'm like, blargh, Gemini! I talk too much, and even when I'm quiet, my internal monologue is more of a dialogue. I have a tendency to overthink things in a wordy, looping, maniacal way.

Now, in the future, if someone tells you that they're a "Pisces, Leo rising, Gemini moon," you'll know a few things for certain: (a) they cry a lot, (b) they like to sing and dance around the house in their underwear (doesn't make them Madonna, never will), and (c) they figured out how to go online and fill in the date, time, and place of their birth in order to get their chart done for free in two seconds. It's very easy. There are tons of different sites that provide this service, but URLs look tacky in books. In fact, you should just go find one and do it now. We'll wait.

In addition to the sun and moon, all the other planets we've discussed have their place in your birth chart, based on the position they were in at the time and location of your birth. For example, when I was born, Venus and Mars were both passing through the constellation Pisces, while Mercury was moving through Aquarius, and so on. When you get your chart done, these planetary locations will be listed as well as plotted on the circular chart. It usually looks like a dream catcher that someone made in the dark.

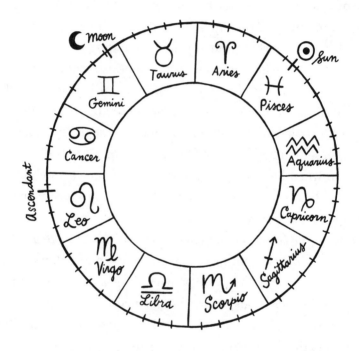

You'll find the planets marked along the perimeter of the circular chart, and lines drawn between them to illustrate the geometric angles of connection between the planets. There are lots of delightful names for these relationships, like quincunx and cat's cradle, but understanding what those things mean is advanced. I am not advanced. You're probably not advanced, either, or you'd be so frustrated with me by now.

Okay! Now we know that there are twelve signs of the zodiac, and that those signs are the names people gave to constellations in the sky. We know the symbols for those signs, and we know that when we're talking about astrology, we're talking about how eleven (or so) planets and luminaries move through the constellations from our perspective here on Earth, and how those planetary movements affect all of us in different, but systematically coherent ways. And now that we're conversant with some of the terms, symbols, and systems at work behind your horoscope and your birth chart, you may notice that we still don't really know how to "read" our damn charts to unlock all the secrets and mysteries of our unique destinies. Radical astrologers like Chani Nicholas are learned enough about the planets and signs to be able to make sense of their movements and advise those of us who don't have their gifts and skills. I don't know if I can mention enough the part about how I'm not an astrologer. I'm just warming you up so that when you discover the astrologer who's right for you, they'll be all the more able to blow your mind. Even so, that was a lot of information. This has been *the whole fucking solar system.* Thank you for joining us.

SUGGESTED READING

Joanna Martine Woolfolk, *The Only Astrology Book You'll Ever Need* (Taylor, 2008)

ChaniNicholas.com

And in Conclusion

I was thirty-five, two-thirds bald, and my bra was/is still often illusive. I was a writer and mom, which is to say, broke and unemployed. And what's worse, I feared, by this late stage, unemployable. Who wants to hire an editor-witch-poet who, if she's being 100% real, hates being awake and accountable to others in the morning? I couldn't say. But I had a spell going. I dubbed it Good Work, and it was just a sigil I made of those two words. I don't remember exactly what it looked like, because I released it and successfully tried to forget it, but soon, I found myself once again crossing the busted threshold of Enchantments. Even before I could ask if they needed any help around the shop, Stacy the head-witch-in-charge, bless her red head, asked if I might want to come back to work, just for a day or two per week, just to get me out of the house, see what happens. I wasn't sure how a very-part-time retail gig was going to help me fulfill my authorial aspirations, but it felt right. You're reading the result.

This experience reminded me that when you have faith that your thoughts, energy, and action—that you yourself—are enough to make change in your life, magic happens.

My dear hope is that you use some of these suggestions to enchant your daily life. Maybe you choose the colors in your outfit to remind you of whatever intention you want to focus on that day, or you perfume yourself with the scent that inspires a certain vibe in anyone within wafting distance. Maybe you'll take a minute during your commute to envision yourself enveloped in the peace and comfort of your own protective bubble, or doodle empowering sigils in the margins of your notes while studying. I find that mindfully taking a moment to ritualize my intentions helps me to will that best, most exalted self into being. Allow yourself to be possessed by your own spirit. I don't always know what I'm doing (ha, at all!), but I have an abiding faith that she does. So as I go through the day I'm attuned for magic, trusting my better, higher self to recognize it when it comes along, whether it's in the form of some gaudy double rainbow or a snatch of overheard conversation that sounds like the answer to the question that's been buzzing in my mind. Magic is out there to be found. It's in you to be found.

Acknowledgments

Thanks and praises due to my family—Noah, my love, who held me down throughout this whole weird thing, and who the hell am I kidding, every single thing. And our Sal, the most magical. Thanks to Donna and Gary Spalter, the most lovingest. Thanks to Ian, Zakia, Siena, Bobalouie, Natasha, Art, and the Spaltini nation. Thanks to Julia Masnik for seamlessly, painlessly transforming from an agent-friend into a friend-agent. Thank you to Caitlin Mckenna for your patience and enthusiasm. My book and I are so lucky to have found you. Your skill, encouragement, and kind attention made more possible than I could have hoped for. Thank you to Caroline Paquita for bringing it, all of your tremendous energy and gifts and good sense, and for being such a solid support and steady companion on this trip. Thanks to Stacy Rapp for helping a witch out and taking me back into the fold at Enchantments, and for being so generous, willing, and supportive of my project and for trusting me to portray *your project* in the right light. Thank you to Mistress Nette for umpteen years of friendship and literally half the information in this book. Thanks to David Scoroposki for sharing so much of your knowledge and experience with me like it's no big deal when it is. Thanks to Katy and Justin and Coleman for reminding me what a tremendous gift it is to be set loose in an apothecary to play and create and experiment among friends. Thanks to Michelle, Carmen, Pia, Ana, Veronica, Jaclyn, Cat, and all of the Enchantments witches emeritus for all of your essential contributions to making a wonderfully strange place ever more so.

Thanks to Chris Jackson for teaching me how to find a book in an experience. You're a true friend and centaur. Thanks to Colin Hagendorf for material support in the form of indispensable advice, always on time. I love being writers with you. Thanks to Anna Dunn for helping me get it started. Thanks to Naomi Jackson, whose faith and support kept it feeling real when it was still out of reach.

MYA SPALTER is a writer, editor, and lifelong New York. Longtime employee at Enchantments, New York's oldest occult shop, she writes nonfiction about witchcraft and poetry about science. She lives in Brooklyn with her husband and son.

About the Type

This book was set in a Monotype face called Bell. The Englishman John Bell (1745–1831) was responsible for the original cutting of this design. The vocations of Bell were many—bookseller, printer, publisher, typefounder, and journalist, among others. His types were considerably influenced by the delicacy and beauty of the French copperplate engravers. Monotype Bell might also be classified as a delicate and refined rendering of Scotch Roman.

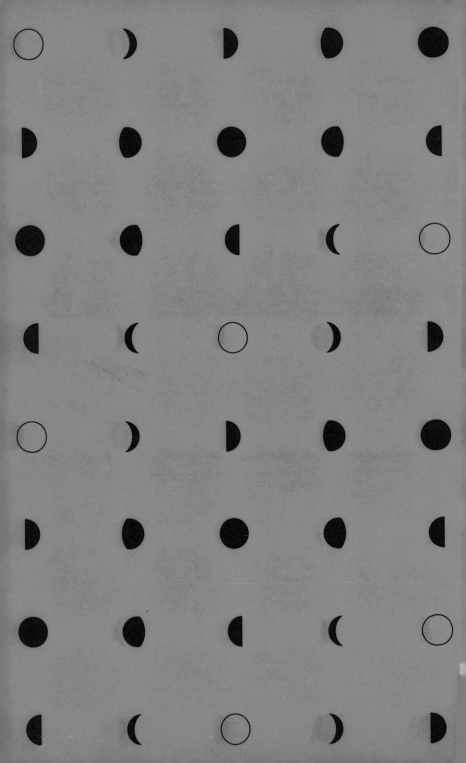